Rate Regulation of Workers' Compensation Insurance

Rate Regulation of Workers' Compensation Insurance

How Price Controls Increase Costs

Patricia M. Danzon
and
Scott E. Harrington

The AEI Press

Publisher for the American Enterprise Institute
WASHINGTON, D.C.

1998

Available in the United States from the AEI Press, c/o Publisher Resources Inc., 1224 Heil Quaker Blvd., P.O. Box 7001, La Vergne, TN 37086-7001. Distributed outside the United States by arrangement with Eurospan, 3 Henrietta Street, London WC2E 8LU England.

Library of Congress Cataloging-in-Publication Data

Danzon, Patricia Munch, 1946–
　　Rate regulation and cost growth of workers' compensation insurance / Patricia M. Danzon and Scott E. Harrington.
　　　　p.　cm.
　　Includes bibliographical references and index.
　　ISBN 0-8447-3932-4 (cloth). — ISBN 0-8447-3933-2 (paper)
　　1. Workers' compensation—Rates and tables—United States.
　　2. Workers' compensation—United States—Cost control.
　　3. Insurance, Employers' liability—United States—Cost control.
　　I. Harrington, Scott E.　II. Title.
　　HD7103.U6D36　1998
　　368.4'1011'0973—dc21　　　　　　　　　　　　　97-25288
　　　　　　　　　　　　　　　　　　　　　　　　　　CIP

1 3 5 7 9 10 8 6 4 2

THE AEI PRESS
Publisher for the American Enterprise Institute
1150 17th Street, N.W., Washington, D.C. 20036

Printed in the United States of America

Contents

Foreword

The workers' compensation insurance system, which exists in every state, seldom makes the headlines except when the system collapses, as it did in Maine a few years ago. Yet buying this insurance (or self-insuring when eligible) is a significant cost for every business. How the system is designed—in particular, how insurance rates are regulated—has a major bearing on costs to business and indirectly on the wages of labor. It also affects the safety incentives of firms and workers. Thus, one important measure of the effectiveness of a state workers' compensation system is the injury rate of the work force. Poorly designed regulation leads to higher claims costs that almost certainly reflect more injuries, as well as higher rates of reporting claims and slower rehabilitation.

In this sense, the regulation of workers' compensation insurance in many states is a perfect example of good intentions leading to bad results. The good intention is to save businesses—particularly locally owned small businesses—from "excessive" insurance premiums through the regulation of premium rates. The results, as this book clearly shows, are higher costs for the system as a whole and probably more injuries as well.

Proving this important case is not easy. The authors, Patricia M. Danzon of the Wharton School of the University of Pennsylvania and Scott E. Harrington of the University of South Carolina, have had to go through voluminous data from several dozen states. But their results are solid and should be of major interest to all involved in workers' compensation. To the extent that state systems of rate regulation produce higher costs and more injuries, they cry out for reform.

What, then, is the case made by the authors? It starts with the "residual market"—the group of employers that cannot obtain normal workers' compensation coverage, presumably because their risks and likely claim costs are higher than the regulated premiums that insurers are permitted to charge. These employers must be insured (unless they qualify and choose to self-insure) and are assigned to an insurer at a premium rate set by the state regulators. Invariably, the claims costs exceed the premiums for this group of employers, and the deficit in the residual market is shared among the insurers in the rest of the market, called the voluntary market.

But this system requires higher premiums in the voluntary market, increasing the incentives for those employers that can do so to avoid the voluntary market by self-insuring. Or the voluntary market can recede for a different reason. As the authors note, residual market rates act as a kind of ceiling on voluntary market rates: severe suppression of premium rates for the residual market to make insurance affordable for high-accident-cost employers "both increases the deficit per policy in the residual market and reduces the rates that can be charged in the voluntary market; this reduces the proportion of policies that can be written in the voluntary market, thereby shrinking the 'tax' base against which the expected residual market deficit can be charged." This vicious cycle has indeed happened in some states.

The system as a whole produces a complex set of cross-subsidies, with some employers being effectively subsidized by others. And because insurance rates in the residual market are controlled and the employer knows that it cannot be denied insurance, incentives for safety measures are undermined. This situation means more accidents, more claims costs, and higher premiums.

FIGURES

As the authors point out, "the major cause of large residual markets is the inadequacy of regulated prices, which prevents voluntary market supply to employers insured in the residual market." In short, price controls reduce supply—as they often do—with bad results all around. Why, then, do the states have these rate controls? The answer is that employers complain about the cost of insurance and use political pressure to induce the state to control the price of coverage. This book also analyzes the pattern of political pressure by employers and other groups.

Once premium rates are controlled, the vicious cycle starts. Again, to quote the authors, "any rate inadequacy in the voluntary market compared with the cost of providing voluntary coverage and the insurer's share of the expected residual market deficit provides a direct disincentive for insurers to write coverage voluntarily, thus increasing the size of the residual market."

Another part of the story involves what is called experience rating, whereby employers with good safety records get reduced premiums and those with poor records are charged higher premiums. Regulatory suppression of this system "acts as a subsidy to high-risk activities and to high-risk firms and industries." A similar process is at work for the insurers, which also invest in loss control—their own form of safety measures for the firms they insure as well as rehabilitation and other strategies to control the size of losses—if there is an incentive to do so. When rate regulation inhibits the markup on these expenses and, in effect, tries to control the return on equity, "insurers may have incentives to reduce loss control expenditures, even if this results in higher losses, because most or all of any increase in expected claim costs can be passed through whereas the loss control expense comes out of profit." From the perspective of both insurers and employers, reducing the incentives for safety measures in this manner increases the likelihood of accidents.

The basic proposition to be tested, then, is that "any cross-subsidies from low- to high-risks brought about by the regulation of the voluntary and residual markets can plausibly be expected to increase cost growth by reducing incentives for safety and encouraging expansion of higher-risk firms." Analyzing data from twenty-four states, the authors find that the proposition is correct. In particular, they find that

· the bigger the residual market, the greater is the subsequent growth in claim costs
· rate suppression ultimately leads to *higher* by increasing the total costs of meeting claims (these effects occur at both the statewide level and the level of the individual rating class)
· in the residual market, where the distortions of rate controls are the greatest, the cost-increasing effects are also greatest

The authors also find that the market for workers' compensation insurance is competitive, so that employers would not be at risk of paying monopoly prices in the absence of rate regulation. Price regulation of workers' compensation is unnecessary and harmful—raising rather than lowering insurance rates and increasing the workplace accident rate, to boot.

These are significant findings concerning an important, if little known, aspect of our business system. The more these results are understood and acknowledged, the harder it will be to defend premium rate controls in workers' compensation insurance.

CHRISTOPHER DEMUTH
President
American Enterprise Institute

1
Introduction

Insurance prices that vary across consumers in relation to expected claim costs provide significant economic incentives for consumers to take actions to control the cost of risk. By implication, the magnitude of insured claim costs and the growth in claim costs over time will be affected if insurance price regulation distorts the incentives for risk control. Specifically, if rate regulation suppresses rates in relation to expected claim costs for some consumers, the resulting distortions in incentives to control costs will increase cost growth. In this study, we test this prediction using data on growth of insured claim costs in the workers' compensation insurance market during the 1980s and early 1990s. Our results support the hypothesis that regulatory suppression of rates increases cost growth, including both the number of claims and the amount paid per claim. While this result, at least in part, reflects increased claims reporting and delays in returning to work for injuries of a given severity, our results nonetheless are consistent with the hypothesis that rate suppression increases the frequency and severity of injuries to employees.

A major implication of our findings is that insurance rate regulatory systems that suppress rates have the undesirable and self-defeating side effect of increasing growth in claim costs. This effect increases the costs of insurance for employers and employees and raises the cost of work-related injuries that the workers' compensation system is intended to prevent. A related implication is that insurance pricing mechanisms that link rates to expected claim costs, such as experience rating systems, provide significant

1

incentives for risk control. It follows that regulatory distortions in these incentives (for example, by suppressing the effects of experience rating) increase claim costs and hence are counterproductive. These cost-increasing effects suggest that regulatory policies that suppress rates and thereby subsidize higher-risk employers and activities have high social costs. Because the workers' compensation insurance market is structurally competitive, rate regulation is not needed to constrain market power and prevent excessive rates. Our evidence that rate suppression increases costs significantly strengthens the case for dismantling traditional systems of rate regulation and allowing workers' compensation insurance rates to be determined by competition rather than by regulation.

Workers' compensation pays for workers' medical expenses and wage loss arising out of work-related injuries and diseases. Employers are required to purchase workers' compensation insurance or to provide proof of financial responsibility. The workers' compensation system and insurance markets experienced considerable turmoil in the 1980s and early 1990s, with claim costs for workers' compensation growing rapidly in many states during the 1980s. Benefit costs per $100 of payroll increased from $0.95 in 1978 to $1.56 in 1989, an average annual rate of increase of 4.2 percent for 1978–1984 and 6.2 percent for 1984–1989 (Klein, Nordman, and Fritz 1993, 79ff). According to the National Council on Compensation Insurance (NCCI), the annual change in insured claim costs per worker averaged 11 percent during 1980–1990 (NCCI 1996). Increases in the average indemnity and medical cost per case involving lost time from work also increased rapidly during the 1980s before leveling off in the 1990s (figure 1–1). Growth in the average indemnity cost per case averaged 8 percent per year during 1981–1990 and 0 percent during 1991–1994. Growth in the average medical cost per case averaged 12 percent per year during 1981–1990 and 5 percent during 1991–1994.

FIGURE 1–1

AVERAGE COST PER CASE INVOLVING LOST TIME,
POLICY YEARS 1980–1994

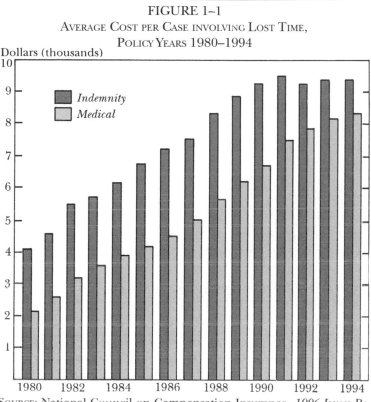

SOURCE: National Council on Compensation Insurance, *1996 Issues Report* (Boca Raton, Fla.: NCCI, 1996).

The increase in workers' compensation costs relative to payroll is only partly explained by increases in medical care costs in excess of general wage inflation (Fields and Venezian 1991). Previous studies have emphasized the growth in benefits and the changing demographics of the workplace in explaining cost growth (for example, Butler 1994). The large differences, however, among states in the level and growth of costs and, within each state, the differences in loss experience across rating classes and between the residual and voluntary markets suggest that other factors play a role.

Growth in workers' compensation costs and insurance premiums during the 1980s was accompanied by deteriorating financial results for workers' compensation insurance. Beginning in the mid-1980s (even earlier in a few states) and continuing until the early 1990s, insurers argued that state regulators failed to allow rate increases commensurate with cost increases. Rates were perceived as substantially inadequate in some states. Insurer financial results improved substantially in the early 1990s in conjunction with rate increases, other changes in regulation, and slower claim cost growth. This experience is illustrated in figure 1–2, which shows the combined ratio for workers' compensation insurance during 1981–1994. The combined ratio is an inverse measure of insurer underwriting profitability that expresses claim costs and underwriting expenses as a proportion of premiums.[1]

State residual market mechanisms for workers' compensation insurance provide coverage to employers that experience difficulty in obtaining coverage in the voluntary market (that is, from an insurer that is willing to sell coverage voluntarily). Consistent with regulatory constraints on rate increases in the presence of rising costs that discouraged insurers from offering coverage voluntarily to many employers, the countrywide size of the workers' compensation insurance residual market increased sharply during the 1980s (figure 1–3), with the residual market share of premiums growing to over 50 percent in a number of states (figure 1–4). Growth in residual markets and associated increases in expected deficits (shortfalls of pre-

---

1. There is considerable evidence that insurance combined ratios are affected by cyclical patterns in pricing as part of the insurance underwriting cycle (for example, Cummins, Harrington, and Klein 1991 and Butler and Worrall 1990). The focus of the literature about the underwriting cycle is primarily on evidence and explanations for a cycle in the relationship between premiums and the expected costs of providing coverage. Our study focuses instead on the effects of price regulation on the growth of claim costs.

FIGURE 1–2
COMBINED RATIOS FOR WORKERS' COMPENSATION
INSURANCE, 1981–1994

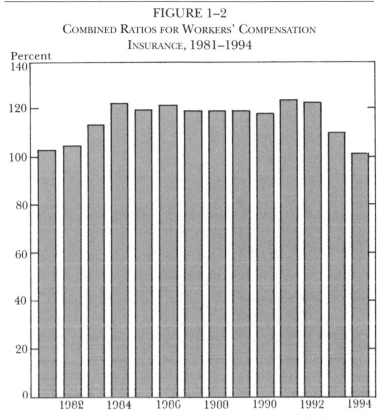

SOURCE: National Council on Compensation Insurance, *1996 Issues Report* (Boca Raton, Fla.: NCCI, 1996).

miums compared with costs) on residual market business increased voluntary market rate levels needed by insurers to cover expected costs (and achieve a reasonable expected profit) for the total workers' compensation insurance market in a given state. Thus, expected residual market deficits produce a cross-subsidy from the voluntary to the residual market so that private sector coverage can remain viable. But higher rates in the voluntary market to finance residual market deficits can encourage more businesses to self-insure, further reducing the size of the voluntary mar-

FIGURE 1–3
RESIDUAL MARKET SHARE OF PREMIUMS AND RESIDUAL MARKET
DEFICIT–VOLUNTARY MARKET PREMIUM RATIO, 1984–1994

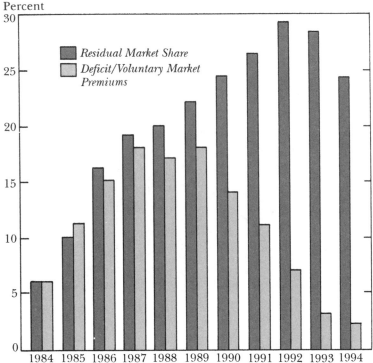

SOURCE: National Council on Compensation Insurance, *Management Summary*, 1984–1994 (Boca Raton, Fla.: NCCI, 1985–1995).

ket. Escalating growth in the residual market and the inability to shift residual market deficits to a shrinking voluntary market led to insurance company exits and the virtual collapse of the workers' compensation insurance market in a few states.

The 1980s surge in claim costs and regulatory responses threatened to undermine the historical basis of the workers' compensation system. Many observers viewed legislation to control claim costs as essential to preserve the

FIGURE 1–4
RESIDUAL MARKET SHARE BY STATE, IN THIRTY-THREE STATES AND THE DISTRICT OF COLUMBIA, 1992

State

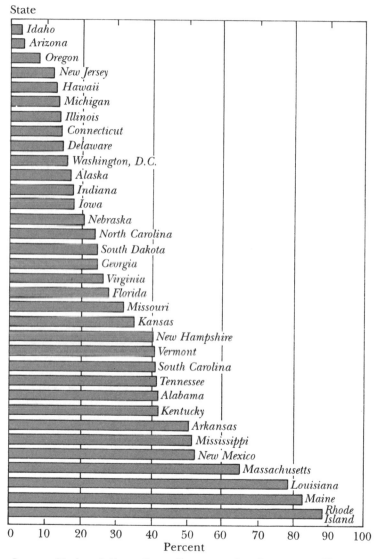

SOURCE: National Council on Compensation Insurance, *Management Summary*, 1992 ed. (Boca Raton, Fla.: NCCI, 1993).

system and maintain substantial private sector involvement in the provision of workers' compensation insurance. Others disputed that regulation produced inadequate rates and argued that changes in benefits to control costs deprived injured workers of needed compensation. Beginning in the late 1980s, numerous states adopted workers' compensation reform legislation designed to reduce the growth in claim costs, and many states made changes in their systems of voluntary and residual market price regulation. These changes were associated with slower growth in claim costs, improved financial results for insurers, and declining residual markets and residual market deficits.[2] A few states also adopted legislation that would expand direct government provision of workers' compensation insurance.

As noted, regulators in many states responded to rising costs in the 1980s by attempting to control prices. Two dimensions of insurer pricing can and have been regulated: (1) the marketwide average price-cost margin across all policyholders and (2) relative prices charged to different groups. The extent of these two approaches and the magnitude of their effects differ considerably across states. While slower growth of claim costs, improved insurer results, and declining residual market shares and deficits in the 1990s have reduced concern and debate over the efficacy of rate regulation, the relationship between claim cost growth and rate regulation during the cost surge of the 1980s remains of considerable interest, given that a future cost surge could lead to similar regulatory responses. In addition, the residual market remains large, by historical standards, in some states, and insurers face considerable uncertainty about residual market growth and future deficits. Moreover, while

---

2. The reductions in residual market size are understated by the data on residual market share of premiums shown in figure 1–3 because of increases in residual market rate levels compared with voluntary market rate levels and the development and growth in the voluntary market of large deductible policies with lower premiums.

the decline in residual market deficits shown in figure 1–3 has reduced concern about cross-subsidies from the voluntary to the residual market, cross-subsidies within the residual market have not necessarily declined substantially.

In this study, we develop models to show how rate suppression may be counterproductive, leading to higher claim costs for workers' compensation. The empirical implications are tested using data at the state level for twenty-four states for the period 1984–1990 and at the level of the rating class from eight states for the period 1986–1991.[3] The possibility that rate regulation may lead to higher cost growth is discussed in Harrington (1992), Danzon (1992), Kramer (1992), and Klein, Nordman, and Fritz (1993), but previous papers have not tested these predictions empirically. The principal finding of our empirical analysis is that measures of rate suppression are positively and significantly related to growth in claim costs, after controlling for a variety of other factors that could be expected to affect cost growth.

Rate suppression may lead to higher loss costs through several channels that are not mutually exclusive. Workers' compensation accidents are multiparty accidents subject to strict liability on the part of employers. Optimal loss control requires care by employers, employees, and insurers. In such contexts, liability insurance that is accurately experience rated does not distort incentives for optimal investment in injury prevention (Shavell 1982). Rate suppression, defined as regulatory constraints that prevent insurers from charging rates that reflect expected loss costs plus a com-

---

3. Several previous studies of insurance rate regulation (for example, Pauly, Kleindorfer, and Kunreuther 1986) have discussed possible adverse effects on the quality of coverage sold (for example, the liberality of claim settlement or other dimensions of service quality). We discuss possible effects of rate suppression on some dimensions of quality in chapter 3, and our empirical tests reflect the impact of any changes in quality on claim cost growth.

petitive expense and profit margin, is expected to distort the incentives for loss control by all three parties.

First, to the extent that regulation constrains experience rating (for example, by reducing the base rate to which percentage experience rating credits or debits are applied), employers have reduced incentives to invest in loss control and to require such investments by employees. Moreover, suppression of experience rating and suppression of workers' compensation rates below competitive levels for employers insured in the residual market act as a subsidy to high-risk activities and high-risk firms and industries. Second, to the extent that the structure of regulation permits the pass-through of loss costs but constrains the markup for expenses and return on equity to a level that is inadequate to cover optimal investment in loss control, insurers may have incentives to reduce loss control expenditures, even if this results in higher losses, because the loss costs can be passed through whereas the loss control expense comes out of profit.

If insurers are not permitted to charge rates that they deem adequate in the voluntary market, risks are assigned to the residual market. Residual market mechanisms generally assign business to servicing insurance carriers that collect premiums and pay claims for a percentage of premiums, with the financial results reinsured among all insurers that participate in the residual market reinsurance pool.[4] Such loss pooling could undermine carrier incentives for loss control, thereby increasing cost growth. Whether this effect is significant depends on several factors including the voluntary market share of servicing carriers and the degree of monitoring by regulators or other insurers. *Insured* cost growth also may increase if regulatory induced cross-subsidies from low- to high-risk firms encourage more low-risk firms to self-insure, thus increasing average claim costs for employers that buy coverage.

---

4. State funds (that is, state-run insurance mechanisms) serve as the residual market in some states.

As noted, our study uses both state aggregate data and data at the level of the rating class to provide evidence of whether regulation increases claim costs. In the analysis of state aggregate data, we can provide some control for the extent to which regulation increases insured costs by causing relatively more low-risk firms to self-insure. The use of data at the level of the rating class within states in some of our tests reduces the potential for bias due to unobserved state-specific factors, such as differences in the mixture of employers and rating classes across states, that may affect cost growth and be correlated with rate suppression. In pooled regressions with either the state aggregate or class level data, we include state dummies or a vector of state-specific variables to control for statewide determinants of cost growth other than rate suppression.[5]

The hypothesis that rate suppression accelerates the growth of cost at the class level assumes the persistence of suppression and cross-subsidies for specific classes in specific states over time. We also provide evidence that class-specific cross-subsidies are persistent within states. In addition, to gain insight into the distributive effects of rate regulation, we develop and estimate simple models of cross-subsidies among firms.

Chapter 2 of this study provides background on workers' compensation rate regulation and residual markets. Chapter 3 elaborates our hypotheses concerning the counterproductive effects of regulation on claim costs and briefly reviews prior work. Chapters 4 and 5 describe our analysis of the effects of regulation, using data on growth in claim costs at the state aggregate and class code levels, respectively. Chapter 6 presents the results of our cross-subsidy models. Chapter 7 concludes by discussing the policy implications of our findings.

---

5. Measures of rate suppression are lagged to reduce the statistical bias that could arise if the degree of rate suppression depends on cost growth (that is, to control for the potential endogeneity of rate suppression).

2

An Overview of Rate Regulation and Residual Markets

This chapter provides an economic overview of price regulation and residual markets in workers' compensation insurance.[1] We begin with background on the basic mechanics of residual markets. We then discuss the effects of price regulation on insurers' willingness to offer coverage voluntarily and the nature and consequences of cross-subsidies associated with large residual markets. The chapter concludes with a brief discussion of state responses to the residual market problem.

Nature and Operation of Residual Markets

All states have residual markets for workers' compensation and automobile insurance. These residual markets require all insurers that are active in the line and the state to provide coverage, either individually or collectively, at a regulated rate to applicants who presumably cannot obtain voluntary coverage. Residual markets were originally developed to ensure that all eligible individuals and employers were able to obtain specified coverage in a particular line of insurance. The traditional rationale was that insurance coverage in these lines is either compulsory or desirable and that some exposures may be difficult for insurers

---

1. See Klein, Nordman, and Fritz (1993) and Klein (1992) for detailed background and analysis of workers' compensation residual markets and price regulation in the United States.

to insure voluntarily because of their high expected claim costs, because of imperfect information about their expected claim costs, or because of short-run changes in the capacity of insurers to write coverage (for example, cyclical effects).

The operational details of residual markets vary by state and type of business. For workers' compensation insurance, the most common form of residual market assigns policyholders to designated servicing carriers, which then issue policies and pay claims in exchange for fees without directly bearing underwriting risk. Deficits for residual markets for workers' compensation insurance are generally apportioned among all insurers that write workers' compensation in proportion to their share of voluntary market premiums for workers' compensation insurance in the state. The state workers' compensation residual markets that are administered by the NCCI as part of the National Workers' Compensation Reinsurance Pool operate in this fashion.[2]

Tying responsibility for residual market deficits to voluntary market share in the same line of business facilitates insurer recovery of expected (that is, predicted or anticipated) deficits through higher voluntary market rates, provided that rate levels in the voluntary market are free to adjust upward to reflect the expected cost of deficits. Given explicit linkage between assessments for deficits and insurers' voluntary market shares of premiums, recovery of expected deficits through higher voluntary market premiums would be expected in a competitive environment (Harrington 1990). If deficits are linked to voluntary mar-

---

2. In most states, participation in the reinsurance pool is voluntary; insurers have the option of receiving direct assignments (or, more recently, applying to regulators for permission to receive direct assignments or have another insurer do so on the company's behalf). Historically, most insurers have participated in the pool, although the proportion of business representing direct assignments has increased significantly since the early 1990s in some states.

ket share and can be accurately anticipated, as each insurer expands its voluntary market writings it recognizes that its assessment for the residual market will increase and will price accordingly. Permitting the recovery of anticipated residual market deficits through higher voluntary market prices is one means of enabling insurers to earn a normal return on their activity in the line and state. To be sure, as we discuss further below, considerable uncertainty may exist concerning both the magnitude of the expected residual market deficit and an individual insurer's share of the expected deficit, given that its voluntary market share depends on the actions of other insurers. This uncertainty makes it difficult for insurers to estimate their costs and price appropriately, thus further discouraging supply.

Rate Inadequacy and Large Residual Markets

As noted in chapter 1, residual markets for workers' compensation insurance in many states grew substantially during the 1980s (figures 1–3 and 1–4). Changes in the residual market share of premiums for workers' compensation insurance reflect a number of factors, including changes in rate levels for the voluntary and residual markets and the relative growth in payroll in the voluntary and residual market. Payroll growth is, in turn, influenced by changes in the number and size of firms that self-insure workers' compensation benefits. Beginning in the late 1980s, some growth in the residual market share of workers' compensation insurance premiums is attributable to increases in rate levels for the residual market relative to the voluntary market (see below). In addition, reductions in the volume of voluntary market premiums in the 1990s due to the growth of large deductible policies have slowed reductions in the residual market share of premiums during this period.[3]

---

3. Growth in residual market rate levels suggests that more accurate measures of residual market share might be obtained by adjusting for

The major cause of large residual markets is the inadequacy of regulated prices, which prevents voluntary market supply to employers insured in the residual market. In a competitive environment without significant regulatory restrictions on price, there is little reason to expect that a significant proportion of employers will be persistently unable to find coverage at any price; that is, relatively few employers are chronically uninsurable. In markets with high underlying claim costs, rapid growth in claim costs, and substantial uncertainty over the likely magnitude of claim costs, however, the price needed to induce the voluntary supply of coverage by insurers may be high enough to create significant affordability problems for some employers and their employees. These affordability problems can, in turn, produce significant pressure for the use of regulation to limit rate increases.[4]

Regulation of workers' compensation rates in most states historically required all insurers to use the same rates, rating classes, and experience rating plans, with rate filings developed on behalf of the industry by rate advisory organizations. These organizations collect loss and expense data from the industry and use these data to develop advisory rates (or, more recently, prospective loss costs) for hundreds of rate classes. The NCCI continues to serve in this capacity in a majority of states. Beginning in the 1970s, some states permitted insurers to file for deviations from rates filed by advisory organizations. Filed deviations, which frequently had to be the same percentage for each rating class, generally were below advisory rates.

There typically are hundreds of rate classes in a state (for example, 600 or more in some states) to reflect differences in industries and businesses. Most states require ex-

---

rate level differences between the voluntary and residual market, a procedure that we use below, or perhaps by using residual market share of insured payroll.

4. See Baumol (1991) and Harrington and Doerpinghaus (1993) for discussion of this issue in the context of automobile insurance.

perience rating with the exception of small employers. Under this system, the basic rate for an occupational class is modified upward or downward based on the employer's experience in a prior period compared with the class average. In addition, in the 1970s and 1980s, some states began to permit schedule rating, again with the exception of small employers. Schedule rating allows an insurer to adjust the class rate upward or downward for an employer in a given class, subject to a maximum percentage (for example, 25 percent), based on the underwriter's evaluation of a number of employer characteristics, such as the presence or absence of safety programs. Until the cost surge and regulatory responses of the 1980s, schedule rating usually produced rate reductions (known as rate credits).

Before affordability of coverage became of paramount concern, regulated rates in most states were set high enough to encourage companies to insure most employers in each rating class. Many rating classes were broad enough to allow insurers to identify some employers with either higher or lower than average risk of loss within the class after the application of experience rating. Competitive pressures led insurers to pay dividends to employers for whom the regulated class rate exceeded their firm-specific expected cost of coverage; service quality was another dimension of competitive strategy. Where permitted, companies also competed with rate deviations and schedule rating. These rating systems generally produced relatively high rates and dividends but relatively small residual markets.

Increased concern about the affordability of coverage and attendant reduction in regulated rate levels relative to the average cost of providing coverage for a class during the 1980s led to significant increases in residual market size, lower dividend payments, and fewer downward deviations and schedule rating credits.[5] Concern with

---

5. Some states refused to allow a component for anticipated policyholder dividends to be included in approved rate filings, thus increas-

affordability also played a role in the decision by some states to shift to loss-cost systems, in which the NCCI files costs for prospective losses only on behalf of insurers, with individual insurers filing their own profit and expense factors.[6]

If rate regulation produces rates that are too low to induce voluntary market supply, the size of the residual market will increase. The size of the resulting residual market deficit also depends on rate inadequacy in the residual market. To continue to write coverage over time in a line that produces a large residual market deficit in a state, insurers must be able to recover the anticipated costs of deficits through higher premium rates (and lower dividend payments to policyholders) in that state, assuming no other form of subsidy. If insurers are chronically unable to recover these costs through higher voluntary or residual market rates because of rate regulation, they will eventually exit from the line of business in that state. Exit, however, may be slow because insurers are reluctant to write off their entire investment in infrastructure in a given line and state (Harrington 1992). Given prior investment in infrastructure, including tangible and intangible capital, an insurer will not necessarily exit in the short run just because rate levels are inadequate to produce a fair return on these investments. Instead, the insurer has an incentive to remain in the market as long as current rates or anticipated future rate levels allow it to cover marginal cost and some of these sunk investments. Intangible investments in customers, employees, and agency relationships may make insurers particularly reluctant to exit a line of business in a state.[7]

---

ing the likelihood that rate constraints would be binding on voluntary market supply.

6. Loss-cost systems were often advocated by regulators and other parties as a means of increasing competition or, at least, fostering the impression of increased competition by reducing reliance on advisory organization expense and profit loadings in filed rates.

7. A workers' compensation insurer, for example, that wrote cover-

As discussed further in chapter 4, during the 1980s and early 1990s, approved rate increases (or increases in prospective loss costs) in the voluntary market were often less than the amount filed by the NCCI in many states. Major sources of dispute between the industry and regulators often included estimation of the trend in losses and the magnitude of various expense factors and the necessary profit and contingency factor (including investment income). The extent to which voluntary market rates may have been too low to allow insurers to cover their costs of writing business, including the expected residual market deficit, is difficult to determine accurately given uncertainty about the magnitude of expected losses when policies are written, the amount of investment income that will be earned from writing workers' compensation insurance, and the amount of surplus that an insurer feels is necessary to support the sale of workers' compensation insurance. Rate adequacy also depends on the additional premium that an insurer feels is necessary to compensate for future regulatory uncertainty. While regulators are unlikely to consider the cost of regulatory uncertainty, private insurers that must risk their capital in long-term investments will generally do so.

When inadequate residual market rates produce large residual markets and deficits, shifting the expected cost of deficits to the voluntary market may ultimately become difficult or impossible. Any rate inadequacy in the voluntary market compared with the cost of providing voluntary coverage and the insurer's share of the expected residual market deficit provides a direct disincentive for insurers to write coverage voluntarily, thus increasing the size of the residual market. Given that an insurer's share of the residual market deficit depends directly on its voluntary mar-

---

age for a business with multistate operations might lose this business if the insurer exited one of these states. States also might take actions that discourage or delay exit, such as requiring an insurer to exit lines of business besides workers' compensation in order to exit workers' compensation.

ket share, the expected additional assessment in the residual market becomes a marginal cost of writing additional voluntary coverage. Moreover, as the residual market grows, the price increase needed in the voluntary market to offset the expected deficit becomes progressively larger, providing increasing incentive for employers insured in the voluntary market to self-insure. This response, in turn, reduces the "tax" base for recovering deficits and thus requires even higher voluntary rates if insurers are to break even. A point can be reached where the voluntary market essentially collapses, as has occurred in some states (for example, Maine and Rhode Island).[8]

During the period 1986–1990, NCCI estimates of the aggregate residual market deficit for all NCCI states average about 16 percent of voluntary market premiums (figure 1–3). This national average conceals much higher levels in some states. The ratio of the residual market deficit to voluntary market premiums is known as the voluntary market burden.[9] The burden represents an initial, ex post estimate of the residual market operating loss relative to the voluntary market base for assessing these losses.[10] Estimates

---

8. If the voluntary market becomes too small to make responsibility for deficits depend exclusively or primarily on voluntary market share, an alternative is to link funding of deficits to an insurer's total activity in the line of business in the state. A problem with linking responsibility for deficits to measures of total market activity, however, is that it can discourage an insurer from participating in the market as either a voluntary writer or servicing carrier. This problem contributed to a crisis in the Maine workers' compensation insurance market in the late 1980s and early 1990s.

9. Specifically, the residual market deficit (operating loss) for the policy year is defined as earned premiums minus incurred losses minus servicing carrier allowance and other expenses plus investment income on the pool's cash flow. The estimated voluntary market burden is the policy year residual market deficit as a percentage of direct voluntary market calendar year written premiums.

10. Workers' compensation insurers are assessed periodically to provide the additional cash that is necessary to pay claims of employers

made before or soon after the end of a year are often revised as more information becomes available about losses and premiums. In general, deficit and burden estimates become more accurate over time. But to make rational decisions about the amount and pricing of its voluntary market business, an insurer must estimate the magnitude and timing of its residual market assessments; that is, it must estimate the discounted expected cost of assessments due to writing coverage in a given year. As noted, insurers face uncertainty when making such estimates about the magnitude of residual market share, the deficit as a percentage of residual market premiums, and their proportionate share of the deficit. If other insurers unexpectedly cut back on voluntary market supply, for example, an insurer would see its share of any deficit increase significantly due to the increase in its voluntary market share. Uncertainty concerning the magnitude of the deficit and associated assessments makes rational insurers less likely to provide coverage voluntarily and more likely to require a higher rate on voluntary market coverage.

Types of Cross-Subsidies. The pattern of cross-subsidies induced by price regulation can be complex. As detailed in chapter 6, to the extent that permitted rate classes are heterogeneous, price regulation that lowers the class rates for all classes leads to some degree of "within" class cross-subsidies: the highest risks in a class are insured in the residual market and pay less than the expected costs of providing them coverage, while the lowest risks in a class

---

insured in the residual market. Because deficit figures include reserves for incurred losses that will not be paid until sometime in the future, cash assessments lag behind incurred deficits, and the residual market deficit has an unfunded component that will require additional cash assessments over time. The voluntary market burden provides an undiscounted estimate of the insurer's total liability for its share of the deficit for the year in question.

are insured voluntarily and pay more than they would without price regulation, assuming some pass-through of the expected residual market deficit. The pass-through of expected deficits, however, is not necessarily class-specific. In particular, variation in the degree of rate suppression across classes—for instance, by altering class differentials and permissible class definitions—could alter the incidence of implicit taxes and subsidies and could cause some classes, on average, to provide a net subsidy to other classes.[11]

In addition to cross-subsidies from the voluntary to residual market, cross-subsidies can occur within the residual market. With higher rates for a given class in the residual market than the voluntary market, a practice that became common beginning in the 1980s (see below), some employers with lower expected claim costs than other firms insured in the residual market will end up subsidizing these higher-risk firms. The voluntary market rate for these employers is too low to induce voluntary supply; that is, it is less than the expected costs of providing coverage including the cost of the increased share of the expected residual market deficit that the insurer must pay if it provides coverage voluntarily. But the higher rate for the residual market may exceed the actuarial or expected cost, exclusive of any share of the deficit. Thus, these employers help subsidize the deficit caused by other residual market risks with higher expected costs. The rate for some of these employers could exceed their expected costs and pro rata share

---

11. Most rate filings and regulatory systems, for example, impose swing limits that limit the maximum annual rate change for a given class due to changes in predicted claim costs. Swing limits are designed to reduce volatility, but they also could increase cross-subsidies. While it is often argued that small employers are disproportionately represented in the residual market, broad analyses of residual market share by employer size (for example, those routinely reported in the NCCI's *Management Summary*) are generally inconsistent with this hypothesis. We find some evidence of an effect of firm size for the states analyzed in chapter 6.

of the deficit if they were to be insured in the voluntary market.[12]

If the separate rate for the residual market for a given class is set sufficiently high to eliminate the expected residual market deficit, lower-risk employers insured in the residual market, in effect, pay the entire subsidy to higher-risk employers in the class. In this case, the lowest-risk employers in a given class are insured in the voluntary market at rates commensurate with their expected claim costs, and the highest-risk employers are insured in the residual market and subsidized by intermediate-risk employers in the class with expected claim costs too large to be insured voluntarily. Here the cross-subsidy is completely within the given class and within the residual market. If insurers could charge a higher voluntary market rate, they could insure voluntarily some lower-risk employers that are insured in the residual market. Without a rate increase in the residual market, this situation would lead to an expected deficit (or would increase the expected deficit) in the residual market that would have to be recovered through higher voluntary market rates. Given these dynamics, depopulating the residual market and substantially eliminating cross-subsidies require both higher rates for the residual market and enough flexibility in voluntary market pricing to allow voluntary coverage of most businesses with expected claim costs below those contemplated in residual market rates. Uncertainty about the magnitude of future assessments

---

12. Assume, for example, that without an expected residual market deficit the full (discounted) expected cost of providing coverage to an employer is $90 but that with an expected deficit the full expected cost of writing the policy inclusive of the insurer's increased share of the expected deficit is $110 (that is, a $20 increase is needed to pay for the residual market subsidy). If the regulated voluntary market rate is $100 and the residual market rate is $115, the employer will be insured in the residual market and thus pay $25 ($115 – $90) to subsidize other employers in the residual market.

could slow the speed of depopulation if these types of changes were adopted.

Consequences of Large Residual Markets and Cross-Subsidies. Compared with a system in which rates are set equal to the expected cost of providing coverage for most employers, large residual markets with cross-subsidies from employers that, on average, have lower expected loss costs to employers that, on average, have higher expected loss costs—whether from the voluntary market to the residual market or within the residual market—have a number of consequences:

1. Subsidized rates (rates below costs) make insurance more affordable for some employers with high expected claim costs that otherwise would face more severe affordability problems. As such, subsidized rates will encourage some employers to maintain workers' compensation protection for their workers and to comply with the compulsory insurance provisions of the workers' compensation statutes. Higher rates for some employers to finance subsidies to other employers, however, make insurance less affordable for these employers. Residual market deficits, for example, cause employers insured in the voluntary market to pay more than competitive rates. Such surcharges on some employers to finance subsidies to others encourage the taxed employers to self-insure, if they satisfy the necessary criteria.

2. As elaborated in chapter 3, rate subsidies to employers with higher than average expected claim costs encourage high-risk employers to expand (or begin) operations. Suppression of experience rating debits and credits discourages safety at these and other firms.

3. Sharing deficits among all insurers could reduce servicing insurers' (or any noninsurer administrators') incentives to spend resources to control claim costs (for example, by encouraging customer loss control, monitoring the size of claim payments, or detecting claims fraud) and

to ensure full payment of premiums (for example, by auditing business rate classes and payroll) unless monitoring by other insurers and regulators and financial incentive schemes are used to offset this disincentive.

4. Insurer incentives to invest in loss control are also undermined if regulation does not permit the pass-through of such expenses, while permitting the pass-through of loss costs.

5. Large residual markets and cross-subsidies increase the risk of a market crisis. As actual and expected residual market deficits increase and the size of the voluntary market declines, the rate increase needed to finance the expected deficit for business written in a given year escalates, reducing incentives for insurers to provide coverage voluntarily and creating additional incentives for firms to avoid paying higher voluntary market rates (for example, by self-insuring). A point can be reached where the voluntary market collapses.

Responses to the Residual Market Problem

Beginning in the late 1980s, regulators and the NCCI began to take action in many states to reduce the size of the residual market burden and deficit. In conjunction with these changes and slower claim cost growth, the aggregate residual market deficit for NCCI states declined steadily after 1989. The major changes in rate regulation and residual market programs included increases in voluntary and residual market rate levels, the adoption of special pricing programs for the residual market, and changes in servicing carrier monitoring and procedures.

Until the mid- to late 1980s, rates for the residual market for workers' compensation in most states were the same as those for the voluntary market or were subject to only a modest surcharge. Increases in the size of the residual market and the associated deficit led many states to begin charging significantly higher rates in the residual market to reduce the size of the deficit. These two-tiered rate systems reduced the expected deficit that needs to be shifted to the voluntary market. As such, the collapse of the voluntary market became less likely.[13] In addition, many states began to allow significant increases in voluntary market rates, which also led to improved operating results for insurers in recent years. Statutory benefit changes slowed the growth in costs in some states.

Other developments begun in the late 1980s included the adoption in some states of new assigned-risk–rating plans that increased rate surcharges for poor loss experience. One commonly adopted program was the Assigned Risk Adjustment Program (ARAP), which increases experience rating surcharges for residual market insureds with poor claim experience compared with the class average. Some states also adopted mandatory retrospective experience rating for large insureds in the residual market. Many states eliminated size-related premium discounts for employers insured in the residual market. "Take-out" credit programs were adopted; these provide a credit against an insurer's voluntary market assessment base if the insurer provides coverage voluntarily to an employer previously insured in the residual market.

In the early 1990s, the NCCI also introduced programs to improve incentives for servicing carriers to reduce residual market loss ratios by increasing premium collections and improving loss experience. One program links net servicing carrier fees to the magnitude of the carrier's (paid) loss ratio for assigned risk business compared with the average for all servicing carriers. Carriers with loss ratios significantly below average receive a bonus; those with loss ratios significantly above average reimburse the pool for a share of losses above the unacceptable range. The second incentive program involves enhanced review and audits of

---

13. As noted, higher residual market rates also increase cross-subsidies within the residual market.

servicing carrier performance to improve compliance with underwriting, premium audit, loss control, financial transaction, and procedures and activities for claim costs. Poor performance can result in monetary penalties or reduction or suspension of assignments.

Other actions taken by the NCCI in recent years to improve residual market administration include strengthening servicing carrier performance standards and eligibility criteria, reducing application processing time, and adopting administrative and educational programs to encourage safety and reduce fraud. In addition, in 1994, servicing carriers began to be selected by the NCCI based on carrier bids (and other factors) that specified the proportion of premiums that would be retained by the carrier in exchange for servicing residual market business.[14]

As discussed in chapter 1, rate increases for the voluntary and residual markets, changes in residual market pricing programs, slower claim cost growth, and improved operating results in the past few years have reduced concern and debate over the efficacy of rate regulation of workers' compensation insurance. The residual market for workers' compensation insurance, however, remains large by historical standards in many states. Insurers still face considerable uncertainty about growth in the residual market and in the residual market deficit and voluntary mar-

---

14. Servicing carrier allowances as a percentage of premiums generally dropped with the advent of competitive bidding. This reduction could reflect preceding increases in residual market rate levels (which significantly increased absolute fees), a reduction in the number of servicing carriers that were awarded contracts (which could produce greater scale efficiencies), and less uncertainty under the new system concerning the volume of assignments that would be given to a particular carrier. The NCCI also filed a new residual market operating plan in some states that provided for prior approval by regulators of insurers that wish to accept direct assignments or arrange for another carrier to accept direct assignments on their behalf. Direct assignments in some states have recently grown significantly.

ket burden. The system remains vulnerable to significant deterioration. A large, unexpected surge in claim costs could be accompanied by renewed rate suppression, reduced voluntary market supply, and increases in expected residual market deficits. Such an increase could cause more self-insurance of employers that would otherwise have to pay higher rates to finance subsidies to some employers insured in the residual market. If so, the expected residual market deficit would increase further, and the voluntary market base for recovering expected deficits would decline, possibly producing a crisis in some states.

3
The Theory of Regulation-induced Cost Growth

Optimal loss control requires care by employers, employees, and insurers. Insurance that is accurately experience rated does not distort incentives for optimal investment in injury prevention (Shavell 1982). In an unregulated, competitive insurance market with good information and experience-rated premiums, insurers and insureds would have incentives to invest optimally in loss control. Optimal loss control requires investing in injury prevention and case management to the point where the marginal dollar invested saves just a dollar of loss expense or provides a dollar equivalent of improved quality to the policyholder.

Apart from the effects of rate regulation, actual workers' compensation markets may be subject to imperfect information, imperfect competition due to switching costs, and imperfect experience rating due to the small size of the employer or risk pool. In such circumstances, the insurer's incentives for investment in loss control depend on the elasticity of demand with respect to price and quality, assuming that insurer loss control affects losses and hence the price and the quality of insurance to employers and employees. By distorting incentives of employers, employees, and insurers, rate suppression may lead to higher loss costs through several channels that are not mutually exclusive. This chapter first describes the possible cost-increasing effects of rate suppression and then briefly reviews prior work.

Cost-increasing Effects of Rate Regulation

Subsidies to High-Risk Behavior. Regulation may constrain the incentive effects of experience rating in two main ways. First, it could constrain the percentage factors, known as experience modification factors, that are applied to the base rate for each class to reflect an employer's prior loss experience. Second, regulation could reduce the base rates to which the experience modification factors are applied, thus producing smaller absolute debits for relatively poor experience or absolute credits for good experience. Given that experience-rating systems generally have been uniform across the states for which the NCCI serves as a rating advisory organization and, until the 1990s, changed little over time, this second effect of rate regulation may be more likely than the first.[1]

When experience-rating debits and credits are constrained by regulation, employers have reduced incentives to invest in loss control and to require such investments by employees. The firm bears all the costs of accident prevention and claim control activities by employers and employees, but benefits are diffused across other insured firms unless premiums are experience-rated to reflect the change in expected claim costs. Suppression of experience rating acts as a subsidy to high-risk activities and to high-risk firms and industries. Suboptimal incentives for safety precautions, such as the installation of safety devices and the wearing of protective clothing or devices, are expected to lead to higher frequency of injuries and claims. The prevalence of high-risk occupations and industries may also increase. Postinjury moral hazards—overuse of medical care, delay in return to work—are also expected to increase in response

---

1. Persistent suppression of residual market rates would reduce base rates compared with expected claim costs, which, in some states in the early 1990s, may have contributed to the adoption of increased percentage surcharges for employers insured in the residual market with poor loss experience.

to rate suppression, leading to longer duration and greater cost per claim than in the absence of rate suppression.

In addition to effects related to experience rating, the tendency of rate suppression to lower the rates for the highest risks in each class and to increase the rates or lower the dividends for the better risks also acts as a subsidy to high-risk activity. The prevalence of higher-risk firms within each class will tend to increase, and incentives for safety, conditional on the type of activity, will be undermined. While incentives for safety might increase for lower-risk firms that end up financing part of or all the subsidy to high-risk firms, the net effect is plausibly to reduce safety.

Constraints on Expense and Profit Loadings. If the structure of regulation permits the pass-through of most or all increases in expected claim costs but constrains the markup for expenses and the return on equity to a level that is inadequate to cover optimal investment in loss control, insurers may have incentives to reduce loss control expenditures, even if this results in higher losses, because most or all of any increase in expected claim costs can be passed through whereas the loss control expense comes out of profit. Any effect of rate regulation on loss control could be stronger in the residual market, assuming that insurers have less incentive to compete on the basis of quality for residual market risks. Potentially offsetting this effect, servicing carrier fees include allowances for insurer expenses that may be less constrained by rate regulation than expense and profit loadings in the voluntary market.

The extent to which rate regulation in practice places greater constraints on expense and profit loadings than on allowances for expected claim costs is not clear. In many cases, regulators have failed to approve requests for rate increases based on trends in claim costs, as well as failing to approve expense and profit loadings requested in rate filings. To the extent that rate regulation is neutral in disallowing either expenses or loss costs, the distorting effects of rate suppression on insurer investments in loss control are reduced. Even in this case, however, some increase in losses due to reduced investments in loss control by insurers might arise because part of any increase in losses could be shared with employers through the operation of experience rating.

A reduction in insurer loss control expenditures due to rate suppression could affect both the frequency and the severity of injuries and the frequency and the severity of claims, conditional on injury. A reduction in injury prevention programs, for example, leads to more frequent and more serious injuries. Less investment in contesting exaggerated or nonmeritorious claims is likely to increase claim frequency, the duration of disability, and the cost per claim. A reduction in an insurer's investments in service quality could be associated with increased delay in paying claims and more frequent denial of claims.[2] While this could lead to a negative relation between rate suppression and growth in claim frequency, ceteris paribus, a decrease in investments in injury prevention programs (and previously discussed constraints on experience rating and subsidies to higher-risk employers associated with rate regulation of the residual market) is expected to increase claim frequency.[3]

The incidence of any suboptimal investments in loss control by insurers is probably divided between employers and employees. Both theory and evidence indicate that the

---

2. Claim denial may be greater for medical claims than for indemnity claims if worker disutility of quality reduction is less for medical claims that can usually be covered by first-party health insurance than for indemnity claims for which first-party coverage is less comprehensive. If employers bear a larger fraction of their first-party health costs than of their workers' compensation costs, however, this differential incentive to cut quality for medical claims would be reduced and perhaps eliminated.

3. In addition, if the pooling of losses in the residual market reduces the incentives of servicing carriers to fight nonmeritorious claims (see below), observed claim frequency could increase.

costs of workers' compensation premiums are borne by employees in the long run (see, for example, Viscusi and Moore 1987; Gruber and Krueger 1990).[4] Reductions in insurer loss control efforts that lead to higher costs per claim and higher total premium costs may be passed on to employer-policyholders in the form of lower dividend payments and higher renewal premiums, including lower experience-rating credits. Employers bear the cost of any changes in these factors from expectations, at least in the short run, assuming that any wage offsets for expected workers' compensation costs are based on the ex ante expected premium. The immediate beneficiaries of prompt claims payment and good service may be employees, with feedback to employer-policyholders only to the extent that this affects their labor relations. Similarly, quality reduction in the form of denial or delay in paying claims may be borne by employees in the first instance and only indirectly by employers through dissatisfied employees. With medical claims, however, denial by the workers' compensation insurer may simply shift the claim to the employers' first-party insurance. In that case, the large, self-insured employer would be directly affected in the short run.[5]

Pooling of Residual Market Deficits. If insurers are not permitted to charge rates that they deem adequate in the voluntary market, risks that cannot obtain voluntary market coverage are assigned to the residual market. Although residual market programs for workers' compensation differ in detail among states, in the dominant model the program is administered by assigning employers to a number

---

4. Several studies suggest that the wage offset and the structure of risk compensation may be significantly affected by unionization (for example, Fishback and Kantor 1995; Mixon and Ressler 1993; Moore and Viscusi 1990).

5. Some forms of quality reduction are constrained by the threat of litigation and regulatory sanctions.

of servicing carriers that receive a fixed proportion of premiums to service the policy (determine the premium, issue the policy, provide loss control advice, settle claims, etc.). As discussed in chapter 2, any residual market deficit (excess of losses plus expenses over premiums and investment income) is allocated to insurers in the state in proportion to their premium volume in the voluntary market. With this structure, the costs of most forms of loss control are fully internalized to the servicing carrier, but that carrier ultimately bears only part of any resulting reduction in claim costs. As a result, incentives for investment in loss control (and perhaps premium collection) may be suboptimal in the residual market, unless counteracted by other factors. If so, this distortion increases cost growth in the residual market, which may, in turn, increase the expected future deficit, rate suppression in the voluntary market, and hence the market share of the residual market.

Whether investment in loss control by residual market servicing carriers is actually suboptimal and, if so, what the magnitude of any inefficiencies is, depend on several factors. In particular, the disincentive to invest in loss control compared with voluntary market coverage will be mitigated, if not eliminated, by a number of influences, including (1) the extent to which it is costly for servicing carriers to distinguish residual market employers and to treat them differently from voluntary market employers, (2) the magnitude of the voluntary market share of servicing carriers and thus their participation in deficits, (3) the degree of monitoring by other insurers through the NCCI and other means and regulatory monitoring, and (4) even prior to the adoption of servicing carrier incentive compensation by the NCCI, the possible loss of quasi-rents on investments in servicing carrier capacity that could arise if poor performance threatened loss of assignments or even future participation as a servicing carrier.

The first consideration suggests that incentives for servicing carriers to underinvest in loss control in the residual market will likely increase as the residual market grows in size, assuming that there are fixed costs of operating distinct management policies for different risks and provided that increased monitoring and possible losses from the termination of servicing carrier contracts do not offset this effect. A carrier would handle a small residual market with the same norms as it applies to its voluntary market business. But as the size of the residual market increases, it is more likely to be worthwhile to segment the two parts of the business, applying one set of strategies to the voluntary market and another, less efficient set of strategies to the residual market, which is not subject to the same competitive pressures and internalization of costs. Survey evidence (NAIC 1993) suggests that most servicing carriers do not use separate facilities or divisions for settling voluntary and residual market claims, further suggesting that segmentation of claims settlement is not common in practice.[6]

The hypothesis that residual market pooling leads to suboptimal investments in loss control implies a positive relation between rate suppression and growth in residual market average loss (per $100 of payroll). While loss per claim (claim severity) is likely to increase, this prediction is not unambiguous, given that changes in claim frequency could alter the severity distribution so that average severity might decline (for example, because of an increase in small severity claims). An increase in average loss from residual market pooling is not expected to operate in the voluntary market. Thus, a positive association between rate suppression and growth in claim severity or frequency in the voluntary market is more plausibly caused by constraints on

---

6. In contrast, a majority of servicing carriers use separate facilities or divisions for voluntary and residual market premium collection and policy issue (NAIC 1993). This result is not unexpected, given that residual market business is not underwritten; that is, the policy must be issued, and there is little discretion in pricing.

insurer expense and profit loadings or by reduction in employer-employee incentives for loss control due to the weakening of experience rating or subsidies to higher-risk employers.

Testable Implications and the Effects of Self-Insurance. In general, the preceding discussion implies that rate suppression will increase claim costs relative to payroll over time by distorting the incentives of employers, employees, and insurers. The focus of our empirical analysis is to test this hypothesis using data on the growth in total claim costs and claim frequency (both per $100 of payroll) and claim severity at the state aggregate and class levels and several measures of rate suppression, controlling for exogenous factors that could influence cost growth. The effect of rate suppression on costs in a given year will likely reflect current levels of rate suppression and lagged responses to prior rate suppression. While it is not feasible with available data to estimate efficiently a meaningful lag structure for the effects of rate suppression on cost growth, our measures of rate suppression (discussed in the next two chapters) to a certain extent reflect cumulative rate suppression in prior years. Given available data and measures of rate suppression, it is also not feasible to distinguish the possible effects of subsidies, constraints on expense and profit loadings, and pooling of residual market deficits. One primary measure of rate regulation, residual market share, for example, is highly correlated with the extent of subsidies and with any effects of pooling residual market claim costs. Residual market share is also correlated with measures of aggregate (marketwide) rate suppression (for example, the ratio of claim costs to premiums) that should be closely related to constraints on insurer expense and profit loadings that affect insurer incentives to invest in loss control. Finally, residual market share will reflect the cumulative effects of rate suppression over a period of years.

In addition, while the preceding discussion emphasizes the possible effects of rate regulation on the growth in claim costs for workers' compensation insurance due to subsidies to high-risk activity and to the distorting effects on loss control, the growth in *insured* claim costs and claim frequency per $100 of payroll and *insured* claim severity may also be affected if regulation alters the proportion and mix of firms that self-insure rather than buy commercial insurance. In general, suppression of the total margin between rates and costs would be expected to reduce self-insurance, at least in the short run before the possible cost-increasing effects of rate suppression reduce the attractiveness of commercial insurance despite the suppression of rates compared with costs. Claim cost growth would be affected if the mix of low- and high-risk employers that purchase insurance were altered, but no firm prediction is possible concerning this effect.

But, in the longer run, rate suppression is likely to increase the percentage of payroll that is self-insured and to increase the average risk level in the commercially insured sector. Regulation-induced cross-subsidies from low- to high-risk firms encourage more low-risk firms to self-insure, while subsidies to high-risk firms reduce their incentive to self-insure. As a result, the average risk of insured firms increases, thus increasing the growth rate in insured losses. Some evidence is consistent with this hypothesized positive relationship between rate suppression and levels of self-insurance across states (see Carroll 1994 and discussion below). There was substantial concern during the late 1980s and into the 1990s that increased self-insurance was exacerbating the residual market burden in many states.

One method of controlling for the possible selection bias due to changes in self-insurance that could yield upward biased estimates of the effects of rate regulation on cost growth would be to analyze data for a common group of insured employers over time. We were unable to obtain the data needed to pursue this line of inquiry. In our analysis of state aggregate cost growth, however, we use the indirect approach of controlling for growth in the estimated proportion of payroll that is self-insured.

Previous Studies

Several previous empirical studies of rate regulation have examined the relationship between the form of regulation (prior approval, loss cost systems, open competition, etc.) and the level of workers' compensation premiums, loss ratios, and measures of profitability to test hypotheses of industry versus consumer capture of the regulatory process (see, for example, Carroll and Kaestner 1995; Hofflander, Nye, and Nettesheim 1992; Appel, McMurray, and Mulvaney 1992; Klein, Nordman, and Fritz 1993; and Schmidle 1995). Conclusions about the effects of rate regulation differ, partly because of heterogeneity in the forms of regulation and because the effects of a particular form of regulation differ, depending on the details of implementation. Our study differs from prior work in that we focus on the effects of regulation on loss costs, use class-level data in addition to statewide aggregate data, and use direct measures of rate suppression rather than the nominal form of regulation.

Prior studies vary in how they define *competitive rating* or *open competition*. A broad definition that has often been used for *competitive rating* includes states that have adopted loss cost systems or allow insurers to deviate from rates filed by rate advisory organizations (such as the NCCI), even though loss costs or individual insurer rates remain subject to prior regulatory approval. In fact, by the early 1990s, few states had true competitive rating systems that expressly relied on competition to control rates and permitted insurers to alter rates without close regulatory scrutiny. In addition, even if voluntary market rates are not regulated, the regulation of residual market rates can produce substantial rate suppression.

Appel, McMurray, and Mulvaney (1992) conclude that net workers' compensation costs (adjusted manual rates) to employers are higher in competitive rating states (broadly classified to include states with loss cost systems and states that allow deviations from advisory organization rates), after controlling for other factors that could affect rate levels (for example, average benefit costs), although results are sensitive to the model used.[7] Higher costs would be consistent with the hypothesis that more regulation is associated with rate suppression. The authors note, however, that the form of regulation may be endogenous; specifically, higher-priced states may be more likely to adopt changes that reduce the degree of regulation. Substantive deregulation could be one ultimate outcome of the process examined in our study. If regulation does, in fact, accelerate the growth in loss costs, as we hypothesize, then states might be expected to deregulate rates, at least partially, as the perverse effects of regulation become apparent.[8]

Klein, Nordman, and Fritz (1993) examine the effects of regulatory regimes on loss ratios, operating profits, and residual market shares, using state-level data for the period 1986–1991, excluding monopolistic state funds (also see Kahley and Restrepo 1993). Four measures of regulation are used: (1) a dummy variable that denotes states that required prior approval; (2) regulatory stringency, measured as the ratio of the filed to the approved rate increase, minus one, lagged one year; (3) a dummy variable for whether a state has a loss-cost system, lagged one year; and (4) a dummy variable if a state requires adherence to the rates filed by the rating organization. Direct writer market

---

7. Schmidle (1995) conducts a similar analysis and provides less evidence of a relationship between his regulatory variables and adjusted manual rates. Also see Hunt, Krueger, and Burton (1988).

8. This outcome assumes that the aggregate interest in reducing deadweight loss dominates the private interests of specific groups that benefit from rate suppression. As a practical matter, deregulation may reduce political pressure on regulators.

share is included to control for lower acquisition expenses of direct writers. The authors find that loss ratios are positively and significantly related to regulatory stringency, measured as the deviation between filed and approved rates, with larger effects in the 1989–1991 period than in 1986–1988. Regulatory stringency is also positively related to residual market share. By contrast, the effects of indicator variables for prior approval regulation are less consistent. Loss ratios are positively related to pure premium per $100 of payroll. Taken at face value, this is consistent with the hypothesis that rate suppression is greater for high-cost states, plausibly because of concern for affordability. The estimates, however, may be upward biased because of reverse causation if rate suppression leads to higher loss costs, as we hypothesize.

Several studies provide evidence that higher workers' compensation benefits tend to increase claim costs, particularly in firms that are subject to weak or no experience rating of premiums. These findings are consistent with our hypothesis since any reduction in insurer effort to monitor loss costs, due to rate suppression, to some extent operates like an increase in benefits from the perspective of employers-employees. Ruser (1985, 1993) finds that higher benefits increase the frequency of nonfatal injuries and increase the probability that a given injury involves days away from work; higher benefits reduce the frequency of fatalities. In an analysis of quasi-experimental data with a decrease in benefits for a well-defined group of workers, Chelius and Kavanaugh (1988) find that lower benefits are associated with lower frequency of injury but with no significant effect on injury severity. Meyer, Viscusi, and Durbin (1995) and Fortin and Lanoie (1992) provide further evidence that higher benefit levels are associated with longer time out from work.

The hypothesis that experience rating increases employer incentives to control costs is examined in several studies. Ruser (1985) shows that the moral hazard effects of higher benefits are less in experience-rated firms. Hyatt and Kralj (1995) provide evidence that experience-rated employers are more likely to appeal workers' compensation decisions, which is consistent with the hypothesis that the incidence (burden) of costs in the short run (from expected levels) is on employers. Bruce and Atkins (1993) develop a model that shows that more resources are devoted to safety in a workers' compensation system with experience-rated premiums than in one with flat rating. Their evidence of the effect on fatality rates of the move from flat rating to experience rating in Ontario, Canada, strongly supports the theory. Kralj (1994) provides further evidence that experience rating in Ontario led employers to undertake strategies to reduce accident rates and to reduce total claim costs.

Several studies have examined the relationship between claim costs and characteristics of workers and occupations, suggesting the importance of controls for industry and other factors. In a study of claim duration in Washington state, Cheadle and colleagues (1994) find that firm size (fewer than fifty employees), high county unemployment rates, and construction and agricultural work are positively related to claim duration, after controlling for worker age, gender, and severity of injury. Fortin and Lanoie (1992) provide evidence on the substitution effect between workers' compensation and unemployment insurance.

Butler (1994) argues that the growth in claim costs for workers' compensation has largely resulted from statutory increases in benefits, a decline in waiting periods, and the change in the demography of the work force, particularly the growth in risky employment and the number of older workers. He finds that both frequency and severity of insurance claims increase as the wage replacement rate increases and the waiting period decreases. Comparisons with data from the Occupational Safety and Health Administration suggest that this is primarily the result of an increased propensity to report claims rather than of a change in workers' or firms' risk-taking behavior. Similar results are reported in Butler and Worrall (1991) and Krueger (1990).

As discussed in chapter 4, Carroll (1994) analyzes the effects of price regulation on the estimated proportion of total paid losses for workers' compensation that is self-insured across states during 1980–1987. This study provides some evidence that higher ratios of premiums to losses increase the self-insurance proportion, implying that aggregate rate suppression might reduce the use of self-insurance. No relationship is found between residual market share and the self-insurance variable. Butler and Worrall (1993) analyze the proportion of paid losses represented by self-insurance for selected years during the period 1954–1982 as a function of the size distribution of firms. They provide evidence suggesting that the probability of self-insuring is a convex function of firm size. They do not explore possible effects of price regulation.

4

Analysis of Insured Cost Growth with State Aggregate Data

As discussed, rate regulation can affect the growth in claim costs for workers' compensation by affecting the behavior of employers, employees, and insurers. Specifically, any cross-subsidies from low to high risks brought about by the regulation of voluntary and residual market rates can plausibly be expected to increase cost growth by reducing incentives for safety and encouraging expansion of higher-risk firms. The effect on total cost growth tends to be greater to the extent that price regulation in the voluntary market reduces aggregate rate levels compared with expected total costs including (discounted) expected assessments for the residual market deficit and, thus, the implicit tax on voluntary market insureds. Aggregate rate suppression also can plausibly lead to reduced expenditures on loss control by insurers, thus leading to greater cost growth.

This chapter presents an analysis of the effects of rate regulation on insured cost growth using aggregate state data. Compared with the growth in total claim costs for workers' compensation, the growth in aggregate insured costs reflects changes in the mixture of employers over time; that is, the growth also reflects a selection effect. In particular, it has frequently been argued (for example, Priest 1987) that upward growth in accident costs can increase adverse selection by encouraging relatively more low-risk parties to self-insure, thus increasing the average expected claim cost for parties that buy insurance. As explained, rate suppression of workers' compensation insurance that promotes cross-subsidies from lower- to higher-risk employers should increase average *insured* claim costs by encouraging lower-risk employers to self-insure and by encouraging higher-risk employers to insure. Whether the proportion of all employers that self-insure increases depends on whether the positive effect of implicit taxes on the proportion of lower-risk employers that is self-insured outweighs the positive effect of subsidies on the proportion of higher-risk employers that is commercially insured.

We begin by describing the data sources, sample of states, and time period used in the analysis. We then describe the regulatory, cost growth, and control variables employed. The next section presents the results of multiple regression models of the effect of regulation on insured cost growth that reflects the combined effect of regulation on cost growth due to its effect on total accident costs and the relative proportions of lower- and higher-risk employers that insure as opposed to self-insuring. We then present results for models that include the change in the estimated proportion of payroll that is self-insured as a rough control for the selection effect. To provide evidence of whether there is a selection effect related to regulation, we also present results of estimating models of the effect of regulation on growth in the estimated proportion of payroll that is self-insured.

Data and Sample

We obtained state data from the NCCI for a variety of characteristics of the workers' compensation market. The most important data are (1) residual market premiums and share of total premiums, (2) filed and approved rate increases for the voluntary and residual markets, (3) calendar-accident year underwriting results, (4) policy year insured payroll and indemnity and medical incurred losses and cases, and

43

(5) average weekly wages and the predicted growth in loss costs due solely to changes in benefit provisions.[1]

The claim cost data are NCCI projections of ultimate costs (that is, projected total losses after all claims are ultimately paid) using data from the first available loss report and first-to-ultimate report loss development (projection) factors based on historical experience. The last policy year available for the payroll and claim costs was 1990. The first year of filed and approved rate increase data was 1983. Because we use one-year lags of many variables in the regression models, we thus analyze cost growth for policy periods from 1984 through 1990. This period encompasses much of the 1980s cost surge and precedes the enactment in many states of significant benefit reforms and changes in pricing programs in the residual market.[2]

The NCCI data sources did not include data for states with monopoly state funds and a number of states with independent rating organizations and residual market pools. Many states for which some data were reported had missing claim cost and payroll data for one or more years. We

---

1. *Calendar-accident year* underwriting results reflect premiums earned by insurers in a calendar year and estimated incurred losses for all accidents occurring within the year, regardless of when the policies are sold. *Policy year* incurred losses equal estimated incurred losses for all policies sold within a given year, regardless of when the losses occur. Residual market premiums and market shares were obtained from annual issues of the NCCI's *Management Summary*. Average weekly wages and predicted cost growth due to benefit changes were obtained from the NCCI's *Annual Statistical Bulletin*. The remaining data were contained in unpublished exhibits provided by the NCCI.

2. This period encompasses the so-called hard market in commercial liability insurance during 1984–1986 and subsequent periods of slower premium growth. There is little reason to expect a cyclical pattern in cost growth due to any cyclical pricing in conjunction with the insurance underwriting cycle. Thus, we do not incorporate discussion of cycles and explicit measures of possible cyclical effects in our models. The inclusion of fixed time effects (time dummies) in our models, nonetheless, controls for any possible nationwide cycle in the growth rate in insured claim costs.

excluded states with three or more years of missing data or two consecutive years of missing data and states with sizable competitive state funds. This exclusion produced a sample of twenty-four jurisdictions (twenty-three states and the District of Columbia, hereafter twenty-four states) with reasonably complete data for residual market share, underwriting results, filed versus approved rates, payroll, and claim costs.[3] Reasonably complete data were not available for several of the largest states (for example, California, Texas, New York, Michigan, and Pennsylvania).[4]

The sample excludes Maine, a state well known for the collapse of its voluntary market for workers' compensation insurance in the mid-1980s. Comparable calendar-accident year data on underwriting results were not available for Maine after the mid-1980s. More important, Maine had extreme values for many variables that were available, and it enacted substantial and hotly contested benefit reforms and fundamentally altered the operation of its residual and voluntary markets with its Fresh Start legislation in the middle of the sample period. This legislation allowed assessments for residual market deficits against employers and contingent assessments on insurers depending on "good faith" efforts to depopulate the residual market.[5]

---

3. The primary data sources included data for Wisconsin except for residual market share. We obtained residual market share data from the Wisconsin residual market and included this state.

4. The twenty-four-state sample includes Alabama, Alaska, Arkansas, Connecticut, Washington, D.C., Florida, Georgia, Illinois, Indiana, Iowa, Kansas, Mississippi, Missouri, Nebraska, New Hampshire, New Mexico, North Carolina, Rhode Island, South Carolina, South Dakota, Tennessee, Vermont, Virginia, and Wisconsin.

5. We experimented with including Maine in the sample using available data. The explanatory power of the regressions declined substantially, the coefficients declined in absolute value, and standard errors increased for most explanatory variables, including the regulation variables.

Measures of Cost Growth and Regulation

Costs and Cost Growth. We used the claim and insured payroll data to calculate the average loss per $100 of payroll each year for total losses (indemnity and medical) and separately for indemnity and medical losses. We calculated indemnity and medical claim frequency in two ways: (1) the number of indemnity (or medical) cases per $100 of payroll and (2) the number of indemnity (or medical) cases per payroll divided by the average annual wage, where the average annual wage = 52 × average weekly wage. The latter measure abstracts from wage growth and is a crude measure of frequency of claims per employee. Indemnity and medical claim severity equals the average indemnity (or medical) loss per indemnity (or medical) case.

As noted, a number of states in the sample had missing data for one or two (nonconsecutive) policy years. In these cases, we used the geometric growth in losses, cases, and payroll to interpolate values for the missing years. The policy years are not strictly contemporaneous, as they begin in different months for different states, but virtually all of the policy years began in the first six months of the calendar year.[6]

Growth rates in average loss per $100 of payroll, claim frequency, and claim severity were calculated by taking the natural logarithm of the ratio of the variable in year t to its value in year $t-1$. This measure represents a continuously compounded annual growth rate.[7] The log transformation has the advantage of reducing skewness in the growth rates due to random variation in losses and other factors.[8]

---

6. For 1983, some policy periods did not equal twelve months for some states. The payroll data for these cases were annualized for the purpose of calculating the self-insured payroll measures discussed later.

7. Our analysis of cost growth at the class code level uses this measure and several alternative measures of growth (see chapter 5).

8. With ordinary least squares regressions, use of the log transformation also causes the coefficients in frequency and severity growth mod-

Regulation. According to our main hypothesis, loss growth should be positively related to (current and prior) rate suppression. One approach to testing this hypothesis would be to use indicator variables for different types of rating laws. As explained in chapter 3, however, there is considerable heterogeneity in rating laws and their implementation. More important, few states had true competitive rating systems for the voluntary market during our sample period. Moreover, material suppression of residual market rates can occur even if voluntary market rates are nominally unregulated, with these regulated rates for the residual market acting as a de facto constraint on rates for the voluntary market.[9]

Rather than rely on categorical measures of type of regulation, we use three continuous measures of the restrictiveness of rate regulation: (1) residual market share of premiums, (2) the ratio of the filed rate increase to the approved rate increase, and (3), although more problematic, the statewide underwriting (profit) margin. We use lagged values of each of these variables in our models of claim cost growth (see below). We do not attempt to estimate an explicit lag structure for the effects of these variables, given limited time- series observations and correlations

els to sum to those in the loss growth models. We note, however, that the indemnity loss growth and medical loss growth models do not sum to the total loss growth model.

9. Based on information reported by Klein (1992) and the NCCI's *Annual Statistical Bulletin* (1993), as well as information provided to us by the American Insurance Association, during our sample period only three states in our sample (Illinois, Kentucky, and Vermont) had rating laws that explicitly relied on competition to control voluntarily market rates without regulatory prior approval. The small number of states with true competitive rating in the voluntary market precludes meaningful segmentation of the sample and estimation of models separately for these and the remaining states. It also precludes a before-and-after analysis of the effects of deregulation. Moreover, consistent with rate suppression despite "competitive rating" for the voluntary market, two of these states (Kentucky and Vermont) had large residual markets and deficits during our sample period.

in the variables over time (and between the variables). Each of these variables (and especially residual market share), however, reflects the cumulative effects of rate suppression over a period of years.

Residual market share (t −1). The residual market share of statewide direct premiums is highly correlated with the extent of cross-subsidies from the voluntary to the residual market due to price regulation.[10] The residual market share is also affected by the extent of any aggregate rate suppression (both current and prior). The residual market share of premiums also reflects differences in the average rate level between the voluntary and residual market. With other factors held constant, states with a greater rate differential between the voluntary and residual markets will have larger residual market shares of premiums just due to the rate level effect. To control for this in the regression analysis and to approximate better the residual market share of payroll (for which we did not have state aggregate data), we adjust the residual market share of premiums using the voluntary and residual market rate differential. Specifically, the adjusted residual market share is calculated with residual market premiums deflated by one plus the proportionate rate differential between the voluntary and residual market. The rate differential was calculated using the history of filed and approved rate increases for the voluntary and residual markets. The adjusted residual market share was highly correlated with the unadjusted share (correlation = 0.98).[11]

---

10. Excluding Wisconsin, for which we did not have data on the residual market deficit, for example, the correlation between the residual market deficit (valued as of December 1991) as a proportion of total market premiums and residual market share of premiums for 1984–1990 was 0.82.

11. Rate differentials for voluntary and residual markets generally were of modest size during our sample period. Preliminary analysis indicated that results of estimating our cost growth models did not differ materially for the two measures.

The ratio of filed rate to the approved rate (t −1). This variable provides one measure of aggregate rate suppression. After making several adjustments to the data described below, we first calculated separate ratios of one plus the requested (filed) rate increase to one plus the approved rate increase for rate increases that occurred in a given year for the voluntary and residual markets.[12] We then calculated a weighted average of the voluntary and residual market ratios, using residual and voluntary market shares in the prior year as weights, which we refer to as the filed to approved ratio. If the filed rate increase, for example, was 20 percent for the voluntary market and 30 percent for the residual market, if an increase of 10 percent was approved for both markets, and if the residual market share in the prior year was 25 percent, the filed to approved ratio would equal 1.11 (0.75 × 1.2/1.1 + 0.25 × 1.3/1.1).[13]

All of the filing information was carefully reviewed, and adjustments were made to the reported filed increases to reflect factors mentioned in footnotes to the data that would reduce comparability between the original filings and approved filings.[14] The most important adjustment in-

---

12. If the state had uniform rates for the voluntary and residual markets, the same ratio was used for each market.

13. We did not attempt to include separate filed versus approved variables in the models for the residual and voluntary markets, given correlations between the variables and the fact that it would be necessary to weight each variable by its respective market share, further increasing the bivariate correlation between the variables and making it unlikely that we could reliably estimate separate coefficients. Klein, Nordman, and Fritz (1993) used a filed versus approved rate variable in their analysis of the effects of regulation on loss ratios.

14. One adjustment involved reducing voluntary market filings to reflect the approval of an "offset factor" for the voluntary market if the approved residual market filing included the approval of a new pricing program that would reduce the necessary rate increase for the voluntary market. This adjustment was made because original voluntary market filings probably were gross of this amount in many cases. This adjustment had relatively little effect on the calculated ratios. Some states had multiple filings in a year. Subsequent filings were usually made to

volved the treatment of years in which no filing for an increase was made. In some states with restrictive regulation, a filing for a rate increase may not be made in a given year because of the knowledge that no agreement will be reached with regulators. Using a value of one for the filed to approved ratio would clearly be inappropriate in these cases. To reduce this potential bias, we used the ratio of the filed to approved rate change for the previous filing if this ratio was greater than or equal to 1.05 and if the ratio for the first subsequent filing was greater than or equal to 1.15. This procedure assumes that the difference between filed and approved rate increases in the prior year persists until another filing is approved.

Average underwriting margin (t −1). Another, but probably much noisier, measure of aggregate rate suppression is the underwriting (profit) margin, defined as one minus the sum of the loss, expense, and dividend ratios for the total market (that is, as one minus the dividend-adjusted combined ratio), which should be inversely related to the stringency of regulation. We use the average of calendar-accident year ratios for accident years $t-1$, $t-2$, and $t-3$, calculated with accident-year incurred losses reported at the end of years t, $t-1$, and $t-2$, respectively. We use the reported values as of year t rather than year $t-1$, etc., to reduce noise associated with immature loss reports at the end of the accident year. The use of a three-year average also is designed to reduce the noise in loss ratios.[15] None-

---

reflect the effects of changes in benefits rules and were usually approved as filed. In a few cases, the second filing was clearly an attempt to increase rates significantly following an earlier filing that was approved for less than the filed amount. In these instances, we calculate the filed request for the year as the product of the earlier approved amount and the subsequent filed request. We did not adjust for within-year variation in timing of the earlier approval and subsequent request.

15. Because we could not obtain comparable data for the 1981 accident year, we use a two-year average for the 1983 value of this variable.

theless, the average underwriting margin is likely to be a weaker measure of rate suppression than our other two measures, given potentially large random variation in claim costs.[16]

The relationship between these measures of rate suppression has implications for the allocation of the cost between insurers and policyholders in the voluntary market. Holding the filed to approved ratio and the average underwriting margin variables fixed, increases in residual market share should be associated with greater cross-subsidies among policyholders. Conversely, holding residual market share fixed, an increase in the filed to approved ratio or a decrease in the average underwriting margin should be associated with voluntary market insureds bearing less of the expected residual market deficit in the form of higher rates and with lower insurer profits and perhaps lower expenditures on loss control. The fact that states with large residual market shares during the sample period generally also have higher values of the filed to approved ratio and lower values of the average underwriting margin (see below) suggests that incidence patterns are generally similar across states.

We also obtained data for loss ratios and underwriting margins developed through 1992 for each accident year. While it might be argued that these ratios could provide a better measure of the rate environment for accident year t than earlier reported losses, use of loss ratios developed through 1992 would increase the likelihood of finding a spurious relationship between claim cost growth and underwriting margins due to probable correlation between loss development after year $t+1$ and growth in claim costs during year t.

16. Holding the underwriting margin fixed, total profits also will vary in relation to investment income and, in particular, will be higher the longer the claims tail in a given state. The inclusion of fixed state effects (see below) in some equations should control for the effect of differences in claims tails. While we could have included a proxy for the average length of the claims tail in the model, this measure would have been time-invariant for each state (or, with substantial additional data collection and analysis, would probably have varied little in most states).

Univariate Comparisons for Regulation
and Cost Variables

Sample means and medians for the regulatory and cost variables during 1984–1990 are shown in table 4–1 for three samples: (1) the full twenty-four-state sample described above, (2) the twelve states with mean (unadjusted) residual market shares during 1984–1990 greater than the median value of mean residual market share for the twenty-four-state sample, and (3) the twelve states with mean residual market share during 1984–1990 less than the median value for the twenty-four- state sample. The two subsamples thus allow comparisons of the variables for states with "large" mean residual market shares to those with "small" mean residual market shares during this period.

The means and the medians of the filed to approved ratio are larger in states with larger residual market shares; the means and medians of the underwriting margin (for year t; the three-year average is not used in table 4–1) are smaller in states with larger residual market shares (which are unadjusted in this table). Table 4–1 also shows means and medians of the residual market burden and the residual market deficit divided by total market premiums.[17] Not surprisingly, both variables are substantially larger in the states with large residual market shares.

The mean and median values of total, indemnity, and medical losses per $100 of payroll are substantially higher in states with larger residual market shares during the period. The mean value of the total loss per dollar of payroll, for example, is 47 percent larger in the states with mean residual market shares above the median value of the twenty-four-state sample than in the states with below-median mean residual market shares. Mean and median indemnity frequency and severity and medical loss severity

---

17. Wisconsin is excluded as we did not have data on its residual market deficit or burden.

also are all greater in the states with large residual market shares.

The mean and median values of total loss growth, indemnity loss growth, and medical loss growth (per $100 of payroll) also are higher in the states with above-median mean residual market shares during this period. The mean values of total loss growth, indemnity loss growth, and medical loss growth are 2.2, 2.3, and 1.6 percentage points higher, respectively, in the large residual market states than in the small residual market states. These higher growth rates are due to higher severity growth in each case. Growth in frequency is about the same or smaller in the large residual market states than in the small residual market states.[18]

Further evidence of the relationship between the cost level, cost growth, and regulation variables is provided by the correlation coefficients between these variables that are shown in table 4–2 for the twenty-four-state sample. These results indicate (1) high absolute correlations among the regulatory variables, (2) high absolute correlations between the regulatory variables and cost levels with larger (adjusted) residual market share and smaller average underwriting margin associated with higher cost levels, (3) smaller absolute correlations between the regulation variables and loss growth with more restrictive regulation generally associated with higher growth, and (4) high correlations between total, indemnity, and medical losses per $100 of payroll and between total, indemnity, and medical loss growth.

Thus, these univariate comparisons generally indicate higher levels and growth rates of costs in states with more restrictive regulation as indicated by larger residual market shares, lower approved rates compared with filed rates,

---

18. The results shown in table 4–1 are for frequency relative to payroll normalized by the average weekly wage. Similar differences in growth rates were obtained using growth in frequency per $100 of payroll.

TABLE 4-1
SAMPLE MEANS AND MEDIANS FOR REGULATORY AND COST VARIABLES IN TWENTY-FOUR STATES, 1984–1990

Variable	Sample Means			Sample Medians		
	24-state sample	Residual market share > median	Residual market share < median	24-state sample	Residual market share > median	Residual market share < median
Residual market share	0.184	0.235	0.132	0.172	0.238	0.132
Filed rate / approved rate	1.067	1.087	1.047	1.039	1.064	1.024
Underwriting margin ($12/t+1$)	−0.235	−0.290	−0.179	−0.210	−0.242	−0.174
Underwriting margin (12/92)	−0.291	−0.366	−0.215	−0.250	−0.290	−0.220
Residual market burden (12/91)	0.171	0.257	0.078	0.117	0.178	0.070
Deficit / total premiums (12/91)	0.115	0.160	0.066	0.096	0.136	0.061
Total loss / payroll in $100s	1.911	2.278	1.545	1.614	2.005	1.448
Indemnity loss / payroll in $100s	1.113	1.338	0.887	0.909	1.055	0.783
Indemnity frequency	0.024	0.026	0.022	0.023	0.026	0.019
Indemnity severity (loss per case)	8,464	9,151	7,778	7,345	7,353	7,237
Medical loss / payroll in $100s	0.799	0.940	0.657	0.714	0.845	0.599

Medical frequency	0.103	0.106	0.100	0.104	0.104	0.105
Medical severity (loss per case)	1,459	1,552	1,365	1,258	1,339	1,144
Total loss growth	0.073	0.084	0.062	0.094	0.103	0.080
Indemnity loss growth	0.065	0.076	0.053	0.083	0.091	0.067
Indemnity frequency growth	0.006	0.006	0.006	0.014	0.012	0.016
Indemnity severity growth	0.105	0.117	0.093	0.106	0.114	0.103
Medical loss growth	0.082	0.090	0.074	0.089	0.108	0.080
Medical frequency growth	-0.018	-0.018	-0.017	-0.012	-0.016	-0.007
Medical severity growth	0.105	0.117	0.093	0.106	0.114	0.103

NOTE: indemnity frequency = indemnity $losses_t$ / (insured $payroll_t$ / average annual $wage_t$); medical frequency = medical $losses_t$ / (insured $payroll_t$ / average annual $wage_t$). All growth variables are defined as the natural logarithm of the ratio of the variable in year t to its value in year $t-1$ (that is, as $\ln(X_t/X_{t-1})$).

States include Alabama, Alaska, Arkansas, Connecticut, Washington, D.C., Florida, Georgia, Illinois, Indiana, Iowa, Kansas, Mississippi, Missouri, Nebraska, New Hampshire, New Mexico, North Carolina Rhode Island, South Carolina, South Dakota, Tennessee, Vermont, Virginia, and Wisconsin.

SOURCE: Authors.

TABLE 4-2
Correlation Matrix for Regulatory and Cost Variables, Twenty-four-State Sample, 1984–1990

	Residual Market Share (Adjusted)	Filed/ Approved Rate	Average Under-writing Margin	Total Loss/ Payroll	Indemnity Loss/ Payroll	Medical Loss/ Payroll	Total Loss Growth	Indemnity Loss Growth
Residual market share (adj.)	—	—	—	—	—	—	—	—
Filed / approved rate	0.54	—	—	—	—	—	—	—
Average underwriting margin	-0.52	-0.54	—	—	—	—	—	—
Total loss / payroll	0.58	0.44	-0.68	—	—	—	—	—
Indemnity loss / payroll	0.57	0.48	-0.71	0.95	—	—	—	—
Medical loss / payroll	0.42	0.22	-0.39	0.78	0.55	—	—	—
Total loss growth	0.16	0.00	-0.10	0.13	0.15	0.04	—	—
Indemnity loss growth	0.08	0.03	-0.08	0.08	0.13	-0.05	0.95	—
Medical loss growth	0.23	-0.08	-0.07	0.15	0.11	0.18	0.76	0.53

NOTE: See table 4–1 for states.
SOURCE: Authors.

and worse underwriting experience.[19] As discussed, high cost levels are likely to be associated with more restrictive regulation due to increased pressure for rate suppression, even if regulation does not affect costs. The regression models we now describe are designed to test for a relationship between regulation and cost growth after controlling for other factors that could affect growth, including state-specific effects during the sample period that should substantially control for any omitted determinants of cost growth across states.

Basic Growth Rate Models

In this section, we describe the variables and estimation methods used to estimate models of growth rates without any control for selection effects that could arise from the effects of regulation on the decision to insure and thus on the average risk of insured employers.

Control Variables. The models for cost growth include several variables that could affect growth rates apart from regulation. Total losses per payroll dollar in $100s in year $t-1$ is included to control for possible life-cycle effects in growth rates (for example, diminishing growth rates as cost levels increase) that could arise from the possible effects of higher cost levels on incentives for cost control and from any tendency toward mean regression in cost levels over time.[20]

The models also include contemporaneous and lagged one- and two-year estimated growth in costs due to benefit law changes using data reported in the NCCI's *Annual Sta-*

---

19. Simple correlations between underwriting margins and levels and growth rates in claim costs will reflect correlation in unexpected growth in claim costs. As we explained, we use a lagged measure of the average underwriting margin in our regression analysis.

20. Similar results were obtained using the lagged value of premiums per $100 of payroll. We are unable to use a measure of cost levels that abstracts from differences in industry mix across states.

tistical Bulletin. We use growth in total benefits, indemnity benefits, and medical benefits in the total loss growth, indemnity loss growth, and medical loss growth equations, respectively.[21] Contemporaneous changes in benefit provisions should have a direct effect on cost growth. Lagged values of the NCCI estimated effects on costs are included to control for noncontemporaneous influences, such as delayed responses in firm behavior or in incentives to file claims.[22] In addition to the direct effects, changes in benefits could be indirectly related to cost growth. In particular, benefit changes will likely be correlated with the regulatory and cost-growth environment across states, with states with high costs and cost growth more likely to reduce benefits (or likely to increase benefits more slowly) than states without substantial cost pressure. If so, any positive correlation between cost growth and benefit increases that otherwise would occur will be reduced.

We also include contemporaneous growth in the average weekly wage to allow for a possible nonproportional relationship between loss growth and payroll growth that might arise, for example, from the effects of wage increases on firm and employee behavior or from the correlation between wage growth and economic growth in a state. We do not make any predictions concerning the sign on the wage growth variable. In the equations for total loss growth (indemnity and medical combined), we also include the lagged ratio of medical losses to total losses, again without

---

21. According to the NCCI, the "theoretical monetary costs are determined in accordance with standard procedures for estimating the effect of changes in benefit provisions . . . as adopted by the National Association of Insurance Commissioners" (NCCI *Annual Statistical Bulletin* 1993, 62). This data source reported total cost effects, medical cost effects, and indemnity effects broken down by type of injury. We used medical losses as a proportion of total losses to estimate indemnity cost effects with the total cost and medical cost figures reported by the NCCI.

22. See Butler (1994) for a brief review of the literature. Several studies have obtained estimated elasticities of claim frequency with respect to benefit levels greater than one.

making any prediction concerning the sign on this variable.

We estimate the models with and without fixed state effects (that is, with and without state-specific dummy variables). As noted, the inclusion of state dummy variables controls for the effects of omitted influences that could give rise to time-invariant differences in cost growth across states that are not captured by our other variables. In addition, the inclusion of state effects should substantially reduce concern that possible correlation between omitted factors that cause differences in cost growth across states could be correlated with our regulatory variables. The drawback of including state effects is that this procedure essentially removes much of the cross-state variation in the data, which can reduce the ability to detect relationships between the other regressors and cost growth. All models include yearly dummy variables to allow for time effects.

Estimation Methods. We estimated all models using two basic procedures: (1) ordinary least squares (OLS) using White's heteroscedasticity-consistent standard errors to construct t-ratios and (2) weighted least squares (WLS) using a model of multiplicative heteroscedasticity (Harvey 1976) in which the log of disturbance variance is assumed to equal $\alpha_0 + \alpha_1(1/\text{payroll})$.[23] The WLS procedure will be more efficient than OLS if the assumed structure is accurate. Conversely, efficiency gains from allowing weights to depend on payroll could be modest if the disturbance variance depends on other factors or if the payroll size effects are unimportant at the statewide level.

Results for Basic Models. Tables 4–3 and 4–4 highlight the key results of the analysis of the relationship between regu-

---

23. The squared OLS residuals are used to estimate the parameters and to calculate weights. Iterating this procedure to convergence produces similar results. An advantage of this procedure compared with simply weighting the data by the inverse of payroll is that it does not assume a strictly proportional relationship. Similar results, however, were typically obtained weighting by the inverse of payroll.

TABLE 4–3

ORDINARY LEAST SQUARES REGRESSION RESULTS FOR LOSS GROWTH EQUATIONS
WITH ESTIMATES FOR REGULATORY VARIABLES, TWENTY-FOUR-STATE SAMPLE, 1984–1990

(t-ratios using White standard errors in parentheses)

Dependent Variable	Regulatory Variable	Without State Effects			With State Effects		
		Equation 1	Equation 2	Equation 3	Equation 1	Equation 2	Equation 3
Total loss growth	Residual market share (t–1)	0.288 (2.20)	0.260 (2.01)	0.233 (1.91)	0.427 (1.91)	0.256 (1.13)	0.477 (1.94)
	Filed / approved (t–1)	—	0.079 (0.98)	—	—	0.208 (2.80)	—
	Average underwriting margin (t–1)	—	—	−0.088 (0.91)	—	—	0.118 (0.83)
Indemnity loss growth	Residual market share (t–1)	0.377 (2.20)	0.333 (1.99)	0.311 (1.85)	0.609 (2.06)	0.418 (1.41)	0.712 (2.12)

Filed / approved (t−1)	—	0.119 (1.23)	—	—	0.260 (2.87)	—
Average underwriting margin (t−1)	—	—	−0.106 (0.81)	—	—	0.229 (1.14)
Medical loss growth — Residual market share (t−1)	0.123 (1.26)	0.115 (1.12)	0.118 (1.21)	0.150 (0.82)	0.057 (0.29)	0.185 (0.95)
Filed / approved (t−1)	— (0.24)	0.22	—	— (1.56)	0.134	—
Average underwriting margin (t−1)	—	—	−0.009 (0.11)	—	—	0.102 (0.80)

NOTE: Loss growth is the natural logarithm of the ratio of losses per $100 of insured payroll in year t to the value in year $t-1$. All equations also included year dummy variables and control variables. See table 4–1 for states.
SOURCE: Authors.

TABLE 4-4

WEIGHTED LEAST SQUARES REGRESSION RESULTS FOR LOSS GROWTH EQUATIONS WITH ESTIMATES FOR REGULATORY VARIABLES, TWENTY-FOUR-STATE SAMPLE, 1984–1990

(t-ratios in parentheses)

Dependent Variable	Regulatory Variable	Without State Effects			With State Effects		
		Equation 1	Equation 2	Equation 3	Equation 1	Equation 2	Equation 3
Total loss growth	Residual market share ($t-1$)	0.239 (2.19)	0.220 (1.98)	0.191 (1.91)	0.451 (2.56)	0.361 (1.85)	0.451 (2.45)
	Filed / approved ($t-1$)	—	0.054 (0.63)	—	—	0.127 (1.51)	—
	Average underwriting margin ($t-1$)	—	—	−0.105 (1.61)	—	—	0.007 (0.07)
Indemnity loss growth	Residual market share ($t-1$)	0.280 (2.19)	0.280 (2.13)	0.246 (1.85)	0.601 (2.62)	0.511 (2.37)	0.602 (2.63)

	Medical loss growth					
Filed / approved (t–1)	—	0.086 (0.85)	—	—	0.161 (1.67)	—
Average underwriting margin (t–1)	—	—	-0.157 (1.93)	—	—	0.010 (0.07)
Residual market share (t–1)	0.112 (1.37)	0.106 (1.18)	0.103 (1.15)	0.176 (1.08)	0.082 (0.46)	0.191 (1.22)
Filed / approved (t–1)	—	-0.001 (0.02)	—	—	0.120 (1.50)	—
Average underwriting margin (t–1)	—	—	-0.015 (0.27)	—	—	0.056 (0.59)

NOTE: Loss growth is the natural logarithm of the ratio of losses per $100 of insured payroll in year t to the value in year t–1. All equations also included year dummy variables and control variables. See table 4–1 for states.
SOURCE: Authors.

lation and cost growth. Table 4–3 shows OLS coefficients and White *t*-ratios for the regulatory variables that were obtained from estimating the total, indemnity, and medical loss growth models. Analogous results using WLS are shown in table 4–4. The tables each show the results for three equations with and without state effects. The first equation includes the lagged value of (adjusted) residual market share and the control variables. The second equation adds the filed to approved ratio in year $t-1$. The third equation substitutes the lagged average underwriting margin for the filed to approved ratio.

The OLS and WLS results have similar implications. The lagged value of residual market share is positively and generally significantly related to total loss growth and indemnity loss growth. The estimated effects are substantial. If lagged residual market share increases by 10 percentage points, holding the other variables constant, for example, the WLS coefficients for equation 1 predict a 2.4 percentage point increase in total loss growth and a 2.8 percentage point increase in indemnity loss growth. The predicted effects are higher when state effects are included. These results provide strong evidence of a positive relationship between lagged residual market share and loss growth.

The coefficients for lagged residual market share are also positive in the medical loss growth equations, but they are smaller in magnitude and not significantly different from zero. The medical loss growth equations had little explanatory power apart from the fixed state effects.[24]

The coefficients of the filed to approved ratio $(t-1)$ in equation 2 are positive as predicted if restrictive regulation increases loss growth. The OLS coefficient is only sig-

---

24. While this result conceivably could indicate less moral hazard in claims reporting (for example, Butler and Worrall 1991), it might simply reflect substantial noise in medical cost growth rates in workers' compensation during a period of rapid countrywide growth in the cost of medical care and the highly skewed distribution of medical costs per claim.

nificantly different from zero, however, at the .05 level when state effects are included. That the coefficient on residual market share becomes insignificant in this equation suggests the difficulty in distinguishing the effects of this variable from the filed to approved ratio. The WLS coefficient and *t*-ratio for residual market share, however, also decline but remain significant when the filed to approved ratio is included with state effects (table 4–4). The coefficients for the average underwriting margin ($t-1$) are not significant (with the exception of the WLS results for indemnity loss growth without state effects), and they have the wrong sign when state effects are included.

Table 4–5 shows WLS estimates and *t*-ratios for the control variables and regulatory variables for the total loss growth equations. (The values for the regulatory variables are the same as those shown in table 4–4.) Similar results were obtained with OLS and White standard errors. Not surprisingly, the inclusion of state effects in the equations significantly increases their explanatory power (as measured by the adjusted R^2 from the OLS regressions).[25]

The lagged ratio of medical losses to total losses is not significant in the total loss growth equations, although there is some evidence of a weak negative relationship between this variable and total loss growth when state effects are included. The coefficients for growth in average weekly wage are negative but insignificant in each equation. The coefficient for total losses per payroll dollar in $100s ($t-1$) has a negative sign in each equation. The coefficients are highly significant when state effects are included, providing some evidence that states with lower initial cost levels experienced greater percentage growth, which is plausible.

The coefficients for contemporaneous benefit growth are near one and highly significant, as would be predicted if the NCCI estimates accurately measure the direct effect

---

25. A likelihood ratio test rejects the null hypothesis that the state effects are jointly zero at less than the 0.005 significance level.

TABLE 4-5
WEIGHTED LEAST SQUARES REGRESSION RESULTS FOR TOTAL LOSS GROWTH EQUATIONS,
TWENTY-FOUR-STATE SAMPLE, 1984–1990
(t-ratios in parentheses below coefficients)

Variable	Without State Effects			With State Effects		
	Equa-tion 1	Equa-tion 2	Equa-tion 3	Equa-tion 1	Equa-tion 2	Equa-tion 3
Medical losses / total losses $(t-1)$	0.014	0.016	0.010	−0.355	−0.312	−0.359
	(0.17)	(0.19)	(0.12)	(1.46)	(1.21)	(1.42)
Total losses / payroll in $100s $(t-1)$	−0.009	−0.009	−0.019	−0.178	−0.177	−0.178
	(0.88)	(0.91)	(1.62)	(7.12)	(6.63)	(6.27)
Growth in total benefits	1.008	1.017	1.044	1.034	1.027	1.005
	(5.34)	(5.45)	(5.98)	(6.22)	(5.98)	(5.91)
Growth in total benefits $(t-1)$	−0.289	−0.266	−0.288	0.168	0.156	0.125
	(1.01)	(0.93)	(1.08)	(0.67)	(0.58)	(0.48)
Growth in total benefits $(t-2)$	0.399	0.400	0.373	0.183	0.175	0.185
	(2.25)	(2.27)	(2.21)	(1.21)	(1.07)	(1.16)

Growth in average weekly wage	−0.054	−0.084	−0.132	−0.268	−0.292	−0.272
	(0.19)	(0.29)	(0.49)	(1.08)	(1.13)	(1.07)
Residual market share (t–1)	0.239	0.220	0.191	0.451	0.361	0.451
	(2.19)	(1.98)	(1.81)	(2.56)	(1.85)	(2.45)
Filed / approved rate (t–1)	—	0.054	—	—	0.127	—
		(0.63)			(1.51)	
Average underwriting margin (t–1)	—	—	−0.105	—	—	0.007
			(1.61)			(0.07)
OLS adjusted R^2	0.25	0.24	0.25	0.41	0.42	0.41

NOTE: Total loss growth is the natural logarithm of the ratio of total losses per $100 of insured payroll in year t to the value in year t–1. All equations also included year dummy variables. See table 4–1 for states.
SOURCE: Authors.

of benefit growth on cost growth. The one-year lagged value of benefit growth is not significantly related to total loss growth, and the coefficients are negative without state effects. The coefficients for the two two-year lagged values of benefit growth are positive in each equation and significant when state effects are omitted. It is not clear why only the coefficient for benefit growth lagged two years is significant. The general finding of a relationship between cost growth and lagged benefit growth might indicate a lagged effect of benefit growth on claimant behavior that is not reflected in the NCCI estimates of the effect of benefit growth on costs. If so, this finding is consistent with other evidence of a positive effect of benefit growth on claim filings and duration (for example, Ruser 1985; Meyer, Viscusi, and Durbin 1995; and Butler and Worrall 1991).

Results analogous to those shown in table 4–5 are shown for the equations for indemnity loss growth in table 4–6. The findings are quite similar to those shown for total loss growth. One difference is that the coefficients for contemporaneous growth in benefits range from 0.56 to 0.60; while significantly different from zero, they also are significantly less than 1. The reason for this result compared with the estimates for the total loss growth equations is not clear. One possibility is that the decline in magnitude is due to noise in the ratio of medical losses to total losses, which we used to calculate indemnity benefit growth from total benefit and medical benefit growth data.

As noted, apart from the state effects, the control variables had little explanatory power in the equations for medical loss growth. We also estimated separate models for growth in indemnity frequency and growth in indemnity severity. The standard errors of the coefficients on the regulatory variables generally increased, indicating less reliable estimation when frequency and severity are disaggregated. The coefficients on lagged residual market share were positive in the indemnity frequency growth equations with t-ratios ranging from 0.96 to 1.56 using OLS coeffi-

TABLE 4-6
WEIGHTED LEAST SQUARES REGRESSION RESULTS FOR INDEMNITY LOSS GROWTH EQUATIONS, TWENTY-FOUR-STATE SAMPLE, 1984–1990

(t-ratios in parentheses)

Variable	Without State Effects			With State Effects		
	Equation 1	Equation 2	Equation 3	Equation 1	Equation 2	Equation 3
Total losses / payroll in $100s ($t-1$)	-0.010	-0.014	-0.029	-0.200	-0.202	-0.199
	(0.90)	(1.23)	(2.05)	(7.08)	(7.84)	(6.62)
Growth in indemnity benefits	0.560	0.571	0.591	0.587	0.601	0.585
	(6.55)	(6.18)	(6.38)	(6.74)	(7.48)	(6.75)
Growth in indemnity benefits ($t-1$)	-0.090	-0.067	-0.094	0.250	0.281	0.247
	(0.50)	(0.36)	(0.51)	(1.31)	(1.61)	(1.32)
Growth in indemnity benefits ($t-2$)	0.296	0.287	0.253	0.302	0.296	0.303
	(2.13)	(2.03)	(1.77)	(2.14)	(2.30)	(2.17)
Growth in average weekly wage	0.182	0.152	0.102	-0.186	-0.200	-0.188
	(0.57)	(0.46)	(0.31)	(0.57)	(0.67)	(0.58)
Residual market share ($t-1$)	0.280	0.280	0.246	0.601	0.511	0.602
	(2.19)	(2.11)	(1.85)	(2.62)	(2.37)	(2.63)
Filed / approved rate ($t-1$)	—	0.086	—	—	0.161	—
		(0.85)			(1.67)	

(Table continues)

TABLE 4–6 (continued)

Variable	Without State Effects			With State Effects		
	Equa-tion 1	Equa-tion 2	Equa-tion 3	Equa-tion 1	Equa-tion 2	Equa-tion 3
Average underwriting margin (t–1)	—	—	−0.157 (1.93)	—	—	0.010 (0.07)
OLS adjusted R^2	0.23	0.22	0.23	0.36	0.37	0.36

NOTE: Indemnity loss growth is the natural logarithm of the ratio of indemnity losses per $100 of insured payroll in year t to the value in year t–1. All equations also included year dummy variables. See table 4–1 for states.
SOURCE: Authors.

cients with White standard errors. The WLS coefficients on residual market share were significant without state effects but insignificant when state effects were included. The coefficients for the lagged filed to approved ratio and the lagged average underwriting margin generally had the wrong signs in the indemnity frequency growth equations. The coefficients for residual market share were positive in the equations for indemnity severity growth and weakly significant in some equations using OLS and White standard errors. The WLS estimates for residual market share were significant when state effects were included but much smaller and insignificant without state effects. The coefficients on the filed to approved ratio in the indemnity severity equations were positive and significant except using WLS and including state effects. The coefficient for the average underwriting margin was negative and significant using WLS without state effects. When state effects were included, however, the coefficient for the average underwriting margin became insignificant with WLS, and the OLS estimate was positive.

In summary, the results reported in tables 4–3—4–6 indicate that lagged residual market share is generally positively and significantly related to total loss growth and indemnity loss growth. There also is weaker evidence of a positive relationship between the lagged filed to approved ratio and loss growth. These findings are consistent with the hypothesis that restrictive regulation increases growth in insured losses per $100 of payroll.

Controlling and Testing for Selection Effects

The previous section provided evidence of a positive relationship between growth in claim costs and one or more measures of restrictive rate regulation. This finding is a strong result in view of the highly aggregated nature of the data and random noise in yearly rates of growth in losses by state. As discussed, however, part or even all of the estimated relationship could be caused by sample selection. If restrictive regulation causes relatively more low-risk employers to self-insure (or not insure) than high-risk employers, the resultant increase in average expected claim costs as a proportion of payroll for insured employers will increase annual growth rates in claim costs. The finding of a positive relationship between cost growth and restrictive regulation is important even if part of the effect reflects selection. It is nonetheless desirable to attempt to test for an effect of regulation on cost growth apart from any selection effects.

Given available data, we cannot employ rigorous methods for controlling for sample selectivity. Assuming that the selection effect is associated with increased growth in self-insurance, however, we can test for whether the effect of regulation on cost growth remains after controlling for growth in self-insurance. We can also provide evidence of whether regulation is related to growth in self-insurance. Specifically, we provide evidence concerning two issues in this section: (1) Are the results indicating a positive relationship between cost growth and restrictive rate regulation robust to including a measure of self-insurance growth in the equations for cost growth? (2) Is self-insurance growth related to our measures of restrictive rate regulation?

Data. Accurate measures of the proportion of total payroll or insured losses represented by self-insurance are not available. Previous analyses of factors that influence levels of self-insurance by Carroll (1994) and Butler and Worrall (1993) have used estimates of the proportion of total paid losses that represents losses paid by self-insurers. The study by Carroll found no evidence of a relationship between the estimated proportion of losses paid by self-insurers and residual market share using cross-state data for 1980–1987 and a positive relationship between this ratio and the inverse of the state loss ratio for workers' compensation insurance. The latter result was interpreted as being consistent with higher prices (higher inverse loss ratios) encouraging firms to self-insure.

The estimates of losses paid by self-insurers and state data on losses paid by commercial insurers and state funds used in these studies are published annually in the *Social Security Bulletin* in articles written by William Nelson (for example, Nelson 1993) and earlier by Daniel Price. We collected these data for our sample period and 1991–1993 (given that changes in paid losses will lag changes in incurred losses and payroll). Before 1992, many estimates for losses paid by self-insurers had few significant digits and changed little over time. Later reports note that improvements in data collection were made in 1992. As a result, the estimates of losses paid by self-insurers increased sharply for many states and decreased sharply for a few others. These large changes when better data were obtained led us to conclude that the estimates in the late 1980s were unreliable.

As an alternative to using the estimates of losses paid by self-insurers, we employ estimates of the proportion of total payroll in a state represented by employers that self-insure (or who are not subject to workers' compensation statutes). We obtained data on total nonfarm employment by state and multiplied the employment figures by the state-wide average annual wage (52 × average weekly wage) to get estimates of total nonfarm payroll. We then estimated the proportion of payroll that is self-insured (or not insured) as (nonfarm payroll − insured payroll) / nonfarm payroll and calculated the annual change in this ratio. We refer to these estimated changes in self-insured share of payroll as self-insured share growth.[26]

The Relationship between Cost Growth and Self-Insured Share Growth. Table 4–7 summarizes the key findings of

---

26. These estimates also reflect changes in payroll that are not insured because of, for example, employers not being subject to workers' compensation law. An equivalent procedure (with signs reversed) would have been to conduct the analysis with estimated growth in insured payroll.

TABLE 4–7
Weighted Least Squares Regression Results for Total Loss Growth Equations including Change in Estimated Self-Insured Share of Payroll, Twenty-four-State Sample, 1984–1990

(t-ratios in parentheses)

Dependent Variable	Regulatory Variable	Without State Effects			With State Effects		
		Equation 1	Equation 2	Equation 3	Equation 1	Equation 2	Equation 3
Total loss growth	Residual market share ($t-1$)	0.222	0.207	0.172	0.384	0.277	0.382
		(2.21)	(1.90)	(1.69)	(2.06)	(1.49)	(2.06)
	Filed / approved ($t-1$)	—	0.057	—	—	0.147	—
			(0.67)			(1.86)	
	Average underwriting margin ($t-1$)	—	—	-0.130	—	—	-0.009
				(2.05)			(0.09)
	Self-insured share growth	0.445	0.449	0.539	0.506	0.526	0.525
		(1.95)	(1.86)	(2.35)	(2.28)	(2.49)	(2.37)

Note: Total loss growth is the natural logarithm of the ratio of total losses per $100 of insured payroll in year t to the value in year $t-1$. Self-insured share growth is the change in the estimated self-insured share of payroll between year t and year $t-1$. The estimated share of self-insured payroll in year $t = 1-$ (insured payroll / nonfarm employment × average annual wage). All equations also included year dummy variables and the control variables shown in table 4–5. See table 4–1 for states.

Source: Authors.

including self-insured share growth in the total loss growth equations using WLS. (Similar results were obtained using OLS with White standard errors.) The table includes coefficient estimates and t-ratios for the regulatory variables and self-insured share growth.

The coefficients on self-insured share growth are positive and significant in each equation. This finding could indicate that a selection effect associated with self-insured share growth increased growth rates in insured claim costs.[27] The implications of the results for the regulatory variables, however, are basically unchanged from those shown in tables 4-3—4-5. The coefficients on lagged residual market share remain positive and significant, albeit only at the 0.10 significance level when state effects are included. There again is some evidence of a relationship between total loss growth and the other two regulatory variables, but the results vary depending on whether state effects are included.

Including self-insured share growth leads to some reduction in the coefficients for lagged residual market share compared with the corresponding WLS coefficients shown in table 4-4.[28] This result would be expected if some growth in loss costs reflects a selection effect that is correlated with self-insured share growth. The reduction, however, is relatively small, especially when state effects are omitted. More important, the fact the coefficients generally remain significant suggests that increases in lagged residual market share were associated with increases in total loss growth apart from any selection effect that is reflected in self-

27. We obtained similar results to those shown in table 4-7 when we estimated the total loss growth equations using instrumental variables to allow for the possibility that claim cost growth and growth in self-insured share of payroll could be jointly determined. We used variables indicating whether group self-insurance was permitted and the lagged estimated share of payroll represented by self-insurance (see below) as identifying exogenous variables.

28. The coefficients on the lagged filed to approved ratio increase slightly compared with the corresponding results in table 4-5.

insured share growth. Thus, these findings suggest that sample selectivity cannot explain the positive relationship between cost growth and restrictive regulation.

Rate Regulation and Self-insured Share Growth. If cross-subsidies associated with large residual markets increase self-insured share growth, there should be a positive relationship between self-insured share growth and lagged residual market share. Absent any cross-subsidies, the lagged filed to approved ratio would be expected to be negatively related to self-insured share growth, and the lagged average underwriting margin would be expected to be positively related to self-insured share growth. The reason is that lower prices compared with costs should encourage firms to buy commercial insurance. Because large cross-subsidies generally accompany large values of the filed to approved ratio and low values of the average underwriting margin, however, sorting out these effects might be difficult.

To provide evidence of whether rate regulation affects self-insured share growth, we estimated models of self-insured share growth including the same explanatory variables in the total loss growth equations reported in tables 4–3—4–5 and two additional variables: (1) a dummy variable equal to one if the state did not permit group self-insurance during year t and (2) the estimated self-insured share of payroll in year $t-1$.[29] The results of estimating these equations with WLS are shown in table 4–8. (Again, similar results were obtained with OLS and White standard errors.)

---

29. Carroll (1994) and Butler and Worrall (1993) analyzed levels of self-insurance share rather than growth. These studies employed a number of other variables in their models. Our inclusion of state effects reduces the concern with possible omitted variable bias. Butler and Worrall (1993) noted that their variables measuring the size distribution of firms within a state were highly correlated with state dummy variables.

TABLE 4–8
WEIGHTED LEAST SQUARES REGRESSION RESULTS FOR ESTIMATED GROWTH IN SELF-INSURED SHARE OF PAYROLL
(SELF-INSURED SHARE GROWTH) EQUATIONS, TWENTY-FOUR-STATE SAMPLE, 1984–1990
(t-ratios using White standard errors in parentheses)

Variable	Without State Effects			With State Effects		
	Equation 1	Equation 2	Equation 3	Equation 1	Equation 2	Equation 3
Medical losses / total losses (t–1)	0.220	0.025	0.020	−0.095	−0.074	−0.096
	(0.91)	(1.01)	(0.85)	(1.56)	(1.20)	(1.56)
Total losses / payroll in $100s ($t$–1)	0.016	0.016	0.020	0.022	0.024	0.022
	(4.96)	(5.00)	(4.85)	(3.82)	(4.07)	(3.71)
Growth in total benefits	−0.040	−0.038	−0.070	−0.142	−0.138	−0.141
	(0.88)	(0.85)	(1.54)	(4.05)	(3.77)	(3.94)
Growth in total benefits (t–1)	0.051	0.058	0.040	−0.088	−0.070	−0.087
	(0.81)	(0.95)	(0.69)	(1.92)	(1.67)	(1.92)
Growth in total benefits (t–2)	−0.040	−0.043	−0.022	−0.036	−0.039	−0.037
	(0.54)	(1.02)	(0.49)	(1.34)	(1.48)	(1.36)
Growth in average weekly wage	0.527	0.518	0.566	0.403	0.391	0.402
	(6.72)	(6.48)	(7.95)	(6.36)	(6.30)	(6.22)
No group self-insurance	−0.011	−0.011	−0.013	0.017	0.018	0.017
	(2.09)	(2.11)	(2.41)	(1.68)	(1.69)	(1.67)

(Table continues)

TABLE 4–8 (continued)

Variable	Without State Effects			With State Effects		
	Equa-tion 1	Equa-tion 2	Equa-tion 3	Equa-tion 1	Equa-tion 2	Equa-tion 3
Self-insured share of payroll (t–1)	-0.149	-0.155	-0.150	-0.653	-0.674	-0.654
	(3.30)	(3.38)	(3.37)	(11.23)	(11.20)	(10.94)
Residual market share (t–1)	-0.053	-0.063	-0.023	0.116	0.085	0.114
	(1.46)	(1.59)	(0.72)	(2.48)	(1.80)	(2.43)
Filed / approved rate (t–1)	—	0.019	—	—	0.037	—
		(0.92)			(1.88)	
Average underwriting margin (t–1)	—	—	0.051	—	—	-0.004
			(2.41)			(0.14)
OLS adjusted R^2	0.39	0.39	0.41	0.68	0.68	0.67

NOTE: The dependent variable is the change in the estimated self-insured share of payroll between year t and year t–1. The estimated share of self-insured payroll in year t = 1– (insured payroll / nonfarm employment × average annual wage). All equations also included year dummy variables. See table 4–1 for states.

SOURCE: Authors.

The results concerning the effects of rate regulation depend on whether state effects are included. Without state effects, the coefficients on residual market share are insignificantly negative, and the coefficient on the filed to approved ratio is near zero. The coefficient for the average underwriting margin is positive and significant, which might suggest that restrictive regulation that lowered premiums relative to costs reduced self-insured share growth.

The results obtained when state effects are included, however, tell a different story. The total explanatory power of the regressions increases substantially (see the OLS-adjusted R^2s).[30] The coefficient for residual market share is positive and significant in each equation, which is consistent with the hypothesis that cross-subsidies associated with large residual markets increased growth in self-insurance. The coefficient for the filed to approved ratio is positive and significant, and the coefficient for the average underwriting margin is negative but close to zero. Neither of these results is consistent with the hypothesis that lowering aggregate rate levels compared with costs reduced the growth in self-insurance, plausibly because lower aggregate rate levels may be associated with an increase in cross-subsidies between policyholders (see chapter 6).

With respect to the remaining explanatory variables, total losses per payroll dollar are positively and significantly related to self-insured share growth in all the equations, suggesting that states with higher levels of costs had greater growth in self-insurance. Growth in average weekly wages also is positively related to self-insured share growth, which possibly might reflect a relationship between wage growth and the number of firms that meet minimum size requirements for self-insurance. The lagged self-insured share of payroll is negatively related to self-insured share growth, which is consistent with a life cycle in which growth de-

---

30. Again, a likelihood ratio test strongly rejects the null hypothesis that state effects are jointly zero.

clines as the proportion of firms that already are self-insured increases.

The results for growth in benefits differ depending on whether state effects are included. Without state effects, the coefficients on the benefit growth variables are insignificant. With state effects, the coefficients are negative and significant. A possible explanation for a negative relationship between benefit growth and growth in self-insurance is that both variables are affected by chronic cost problems that are not captured by the other variables. Specifically, states with chronic cost problems could experience larger growth in self-insurance and be less likely to increase benefits (and more likely to decrease benefits).

The coefficients for the no-group self-insurance dummy variable are negative and significant without state effects, but they are positive and weakly significant with state effects. Intuition suggests a negative relationship. Carroll (1994) found a negative relationship between no-group self-insurance and the ratio of estimated self-insured paid losses to total paid losses, and Butler and Worrall (1993) report a small positive effect on this ratio of laws that permit group self-insurance. When state effects are included, however, the coefficients on this variable reflect differences in growth rates for states that began to permit group self-insurance compared with states that did not change their regulations. The effects of these regulations for states with constant regimes will be impounded in the state effects. A positive relationship between the no-group self-insurance variable and growth in self-insurance could arise if states with larger self-insurance growth for reasons not captured by the other variables were more likely to permit group self-insurance first during this period.

As noted, the key results for the regulatory variables depend on whether state effects are included. With state effects, the results suggest that policies that led to large residual market shares increased growth in self-insurance. Thus, these results are consistent with concern over a possible death spiral in the insured market. Without state effects, there is no significant relationship between lagged residual market share and self-insured share growth, and there is some evidence that policies that reduced average underwriting margins slowed self-insurance growth.

Which equations are more reliable, those with state effects or those without? Omission from the equations of many factors that could influence growth in self-insurance, such as employer size and differences in requirements to qualify as a self-insurer, favors including fixed state effects to control for possible omitted variable bias. Consistent with omitted factors, including fixed state effects leads to a large increase in the explanatory power of the equations as was noted earlier.

Conclusions

The overarching results of our analysis of state aggregate cost growth are consistent with the hypothesis that rate suppression increases growth in claim costs. In particular, we find evidence that lagged residual market share is positively and significantly related to total cost growth and indemnity cost growth. This positive effect remains when growth in the estimated proportion of payroll that is self-insured is included in the models as a control for the selection effect that arises if rate suppression increases (decreases) the proportion of lower- (higher-) risk employers that self-insure. Our results also are consistent with the hypothesis that rate suppression increases growth in self-insurance when state effects are included in the model to control for omitted state influences.

5
Analysis of Cost Growth
with Class Data

This chapter examines the effects of rate regulation on cost growth at the level of the individual rating class in eight states for which we obtained class level data. The evidence shows considerable variation in both the level and the growth of loss costs across rating classes in each state; for each class, losses and loss growth often differ between the residual and voluntary markets. The mean loss per $100 payroll, for example, calculated as the unweighted average of the means for each class, ranges from $3.62 in Virginia to $16.70 in Maine for the voluntary market; for the residual market, the mean loss per $100 payroll ranges from $8.92 in Illinois to $22.60 in Florida.

The theory outlined in chapter 3 implies that classes or subclasses for which rates are persistently below fair levels are expected to experience more rapid growth in costs than classes or subclasses that pay adequate or excessive rates. Subsidized rates and the suppression of experience rating are likely to undermine incentives for loss control on the part of employers, employees, and insurers. The positive association between rate suppression and cost growth due to these effects of moral hazard is expected to be greater in the residual market than in the voluntary market because rate suppression is greater and affects a larger share of the market. These effects could be exacerbated if servicing carriers have little incentive to invest in loss control as a form of price and quality competition or if pooling of losses in the residual market leads to suboptimal insurer investments in loss control. Any incentive for servicing carriers to underinvest in loss control could increase as the residual market grows in size because the development of separate management strategies for the voluntary and residual markets may then become more worthwhile.

In chapter 4, we showed that the predicted positive relationship between rate suppression and cost growth is observed in statewide, aggregate data. To test whether this relationship also occurs at the class and subclass levels, in this chapter we report analysis of cost growth by class for the top 150 classes in each state. Results are reported for the total market and for the voluntary and residual markets separately.

Data and Methods

The data are from the NCCI for eight states that represent a range of regulatory regimes. The data are reported by individual rating class for the 150 largest classes in each state for the five policy years 1987–1991. These data distinguish voluntary market and residual market experience for each class. For each policy year, we use the fully developed value of claims and losses based on the most recent report available, to ensure comparability across policy years.[1] We convert all dollar values to constant 1992 dollars using a wage index for payroll and indemnity losses, a medical index for medical losses, and a weighted average of the medical and wage indexes for premiums.[2] Of the 150 class codes,

---

1. Since the development factors are uniform for all classes in a state, the use of fully developed losses may obscure differences in payout tails across classes. Our estimates of ultimate losses may be more accurate for earlier policy years, for which the reported loss data are more mature than for more recent policy years. Provided that resulting error is random across classes and states, our estimates should be unbiased.

2. We employ constant dollar amounts given our use of multiyear means to measure loss growth (see below).

64 are common to all eight states, 25 are in seven states, and 120 are present in only one state. Although these 150 classes represent only roughly one-third of the classes in each state, they account for over 80 percent of the market as measured by risks, premium, payroll, and losses.

Rating classes are defined roughly along occupational lines. Manual rates are expressed per $100 of payroll. The rate for a specific employer-policyholder ("the risk") is the payroll-weighted average of rates for the classes represented by its employees. The class data on premiums, losses, payroll, etc., reflect the pooled experience for that class from all employers that employ the class in the state.[3] These data do not distinguish experience of individual employer-policyholders or insurers within a class. The database reports each employer as a risk in the class that represents the dominant share of its payroll. Thus, the count of risks per class is a count of firms for which that class is the dominant class, by share of payroll.

The loss data at the class level exhibit extreme stochastic variation across years; payroll and number of risks are also unstable because of such factors as employer switching to self-insurance or employment changes that alter the class mix and hence affect the classification of firms by dominant class. This instability makes estimates based on year-to-year trends imprecise. Here we use multiyear mean values that average out some of the stochastic variation.[4] Specifically, the growth in losses is defined as the change between the mean for the most recent three policy years and the prior two policy years.

We consider three measures of cost growth: absolute growth in costs, simple percentage cost growth, and the natural logarithm of percentage cost growth, which is also

---

3. Large states are largely self-rated, but the experience of smaller states may be pooled in the NCCI rating procedure (Gogol 1985).

4. Means are weighted means; that is, the three-year mean loss per $100 payroll is the sum of losses divided by the sum of payroll.

used in chapter 4.[5] Because our data are not an annual time series, the log percentage growth is not a precise measure of continuously compounded growth, as it is in chapter 4. These different measures could result in different conclusions. Classes with a relatively high initial level of costs, for example, could experience more rapid growth in absolute dollars per $100 payroll than classes that start from a lower level, but the high-cost class could still have a lower percentage growth rate because of the higher starting point.[6] The absolute growth measure could thus detect effects that are masked in the measures of percentage growth. An advantage of the measure of log growth is that the growth in total loss is equal to the sum of the growth in claim frequency and severity.

Our measure of rate suppression at the class level is the lagged class-specific percentage of payroll in the residual market. This is the best available class-specific measure of the percentage of employees for whom voluntary market rates are perceived to be inadequate either because of suppression of voluntary market rates or because of suppression of residual market rates, which then set a ceiling on the rates that can be charged in the voluntary market.[7] The regulatory stringency measure (ratio of filed to approved rates) is not available at the class level. Even if it were, it would, at best, reflect only a mean estimate of rate inadequacy for the class; it would not reflect the percent-

---

5. Let Y_t denote the mean for the most recent three policy years, Y_{t-1} denotes the mean for the prior two years. Then absolute cost growth is $Y_t - Y_{t-1}$, percentage cost growth is $(Y_t / Y_{t-1} - 1)$, and the natural log of percentage cost growth is $\ln(Y_t / Y_{t-1})$.

6. We allow for this possibility in the analysis of state aggregate data in chapter 4 by including lagged costs per payroll dollar.

7. It is also sometimes said that insurers assign some high-risk firms, particularly small firms, to the residual market because of uncertainty. This may reflect a reluctance to charge a rate that the insurer considers adequate, for political reasons or because it would obviously be unaffordable.

age of the class for whom rates are inadequate, which is captured by residual market share of payroll. The lagged value is an average over the earliest two-year time period, which is the base period for our growth measures. We present evidence below that the three possible measures of residual market share—based on payroll, premiums, and risks—are highly correlated. Here we use percentage of payroll as the most accurate measure of insurer exposure and of number of employees in the residual market.[8]

To test the hypothesis that insurer response is increasing in the magnitude of the residual market deficit, in some equations we include the lagged residual market deficit per $100 payroll in the state, which reflects both the share of payroll in the residual market and the ex post magnitude of rate inadequacy per unit of payroll for the state as a whole. In the preliminary analysis, we also used the statewide mean residual market share of payroll (the payroll-weighted average of the class-specific shares of payroll in the residual market). This measure was generally insignificant or negative, contrary to expectations, possibly because it is highly correlated (0.82) with the class-specific residual market share. The correlation between residual market deficit and class-specific residual market share is 0.45 (excluding Maine). The statewide ratio of filed to approved rate in-

---

8. Since we do not have the residual market share of payroll for the analysis of state aggregate data in chapter 4, we adjusted the residual market share of premiums using the rate differential between the voluntary and residual markets to approximate a payroll-based measure. The percentage of risks is not weighted to reflect differences across classes in the average number of employees per risk. The percentage of payroll is a biased measure of the percentage of employees to the extent that average payroll per employee differs between the residual and the voluntary markets. Since rates are based on payroll, not employees, however, payroll is the relevant measure for insurer incentives. As noted, growth in large deductible policies in the voluntary market, which alters the interpretation of the residual market share of either premiums or payroll, generally took place after our sample period.

creases was also generally insignificant. Because all these measures are marketwide averages, they may be inaccurately measured for specific classes, which may contribute to the finding of no significant effect.

We use the lagged value of the residual market share in the cost growth regressions as an instrument for contemporaneous residual market share, which should reflect the cumulative effects of rate suppression. Use of the contemporaneous residual market share could result in endogeneity bias because insurers' current residual market allocation decisions are themselves influenced by expected loss costs, relative to premium. To the extent that the lagged residual market share is an imprecise measure of contemporaneous residual market share because of both the lag and the averaging across years, the resulting measurement error reduces the precision of coefficient estimates, leading to downward biased estimates of statistical significance.[9]

To identify the effects of rate suppression, it is essential to control for other factors that may independently influence cost growth and that are correlated with rate suppression. For these class-level data, the available information is more limited than for the state-level analysis reported in chapter 4. We include a vector of industry dummy variables to control for industry-specific influences on loss costs.[10] The lagged predicted percentage change in loss costs for the state, as estimated by the NCCI, is included to control for effects of statutory benefit changes on costs. The

---

9. If there is a positive causal relation from loss in year t to residual market share in year t, then since loss in $t-1$ appears in the denominator of the dependent variable, it would be positively correlated with the explanatory variable, residual market share in $t-1$, which would bias down the estimated effect on loss growth. Thus, if there is reverse causation, our specification will yield lower bound estimates of the effect of residual market share on loss growth.

10. The industry classification is defined by NCCI. It is similar but not identical to the SIC classification.

estimated effects of this variable on loss growth may underestimate the true effect to the extent that states with adverse insurance market experience—high and rapidly growing costs, large residual markets, declining availability in the voluntary market—are more likely to adopt statutory benefit changes.

Since these observed state-specific variables do not control for all the possible state characteristics that influence loss growth, their coefficient estimates may be biased. In some specifications, we substitute a vector of state dummy variables to control for all state differences.[11]

The theoretical model pertains to the effect of rate suppression on loss growth for a group of policies with specified risk characteristics. The observed measures of loss growth in the voluntary and residual markets are likely to be downward (upward) biased if the residual market is growing (shrinking). As the residual market grows, the marginal risk has lower expected costs than the average risk, leading to a downward biased measure of mean loss in the residual market, assuming that higher risks are the first to be assigned to the residual market. A similar downward bias in estimated loss growth occurs in the voluntary market because the average expected loss per exposure unit declines as the voluntary market shrinks, assuming that the lowest risks are the last to be shifted to the residual market. In some equations, we therefore include the growth in the residual market share to control for selection bias due to the shifting of risks between the voluntary and residual markets. Including this control is expected to increase the estimated effect of rate suppression on cost growth. The selection bias due to shifting of risks between the voluntary and residual markets should not affect estimates of cost growth for the class as a whole, averaging over volun-

---

11. The standard errors for the state-specific variables may be biased downward because of our combination of state aggregate explanatory variables with class-level dependent variables (see Moulton 1990).

tary and residual markets, if the exposure base is unchanged over time.

In reality, however, rate suppression and a growing residual market tend to increase the burden or deficit tax on voluntary market premiums and hence increase the incentives of lower-risk employers to switch to self-insurance. As discussed in chapter 4, the self-selection of lower risks to self-insurance can lead to upward-biased estimates of rate suppression on insured loss growth. This upward bias in unconditional estimates of the effect of rate suppression on marketwide loss growth due to self-insurance is greatest where rate suppression is concentrated on residual market premiums since that tends to increase the implicit tax on premiums charged in the voluntary market. Holding the expected deficit constant, our measure of rate suppression—the residual market share of payroll—may primarily reflect rate suppression in the voluntary market. Since this reduces the cost of market insurance relative to self-insurance and hence reduces incentives to self-insure, the net bias in the coefficient estimates may be small in our equations that also include the statewide residual market deficit.

As in the analysis of state aggregate cost growth, we exclude Maine from the analysis at the class code level because its abnormally large residual market size suggests that its experience is atypical and could bias conclusions for other states. In fact, including Maine generally results in similar but less precise coefficient estimates. We exclude from the regression analysis observations with missing data on premiums or payroll. We also exclude observations for which any loss growth measures (absolute, relative, and percentage growth in total losses, claim frequency, or severity) were more than four standard deviations from the mean for that variable. Such extreme deviations reflect the stochastic variation in losses at the class level that remains even after averaging the class experience across years. This reduced the sample from 1,050 (after omitting Maine) to

860 observations. We report results using OLS with approximate t-statistics based on White standard errors to adjust for heteroscedasticity in estimates.[12]

Empirical Results

Rate Suppression, Cost Levels, and Growth Rates by Market Segment. Table 5–1 reports several measures of mean statewide rate suppression for each of the eight states: the residual market share of premiums, payroll and risks, the loss ratio, the statewide ratio of filed to approved rates, and the residual market deficit per $100 of payroll. The loss ratio for each state is the unweighted mean across classes, where each class-specific mean is the five-year mean of losses divided by the five-year mean of standard premiums.

The mean residual market share of payroll is similar to the share of premium but consistently less than the share of risks. This implies that firms in the residual market, on average, have lower payroll than firms in the voluntary market, either because of fewer employees or because of lower wages. The ranking by loss ratios is similar to the rankings by residual market shares. The ranking by ratio of filed to approved rates (regulatory stringency) is less consistent, possibly because regulatory stringency reflects the magnitude of the difference between filed and approved rates rather than the percentage of payroll for which the filed rates are inadequate.

Table 5–2 compares claim frequency, claim severity, and total loss per dollar of payroll for the voluntary and residual markets in each state for the early and later time periods. The observation for each class is the weighted mean over years 1–3 or 4–5, and the market mean is the unweighted mean across classes. The weighted mean loss per $100 of payroll, defined as the ratio of marketwide loss

---

12. Results were similar using weighted least squares with the square root of payroll as the weight.

TABLE 5-1
MEASURES OF RATE SUPPRESSION BY STATE,
FIVE-YEAR MEANS, 1986–1991

State	Share of the Residual Market								Loss Ratio	Rank	Filed/ Approved Volun- tary	Rank	Filed/ Approved Resid- ual	Rank	Filed/ Approved Ave- rage	Rank
	Pay- roll	Rank	Risks	Rank	Pre- mium	Rank										
Michigan	0.060	1	0.124	1	0.076	1	0.828	2	1.007	2	1.013	1	1.008	1
Georgia	0.111	2	0.248	2	0.158	2	0.922	4	1.080	4	1.699	7	1.180	5
Illinois	0.115	3	0.260	3	0.141	3	0.681	1	1.000	1	1.167	4	1.027	2
Virginia	0.135	4	0.289	4	0.149	4	0.916	3	1.201	6	1.210	5	1.203	6
Alabama	0.212	5	0.387	5	0.228	5	1.139	6	1.065	3	1.060	3	1.064	3
Florida	0.220	6	0.513	6	0.208	6	1.381	8	1.138	5	1.050	2	1.118	4
Louisiana	0.364	7	0.562	7	0.397	7	1.053	5	1.322	7	1.350	6	1.339	7
Maine	0.775	8	0.869	8	0.787	8	1.306	7	1.569	8	1.863	8	1.771	8

NOTE: See text for definition of five-year means.
SOURCE: Authors.

to marketwide premium, is also reported. This is the measure frequently cited in other studies; it indicates the aggregate experience for the state under the assumption that unrestricted cross-subsidization across classes is feasible within the voluntary and residual markets, respectively.

In all states except Maine, both claim frequency and total loss per $100 of payroll are significantly higher in the residual market than in the voluntary market. Claim severity is also higher in the residual markets than in the voluntary markets, except in Alabama, Louisiana, and Maine. Maine is anomalous in having the greatest residual market share (78 percent of payroll, 79 percent of premium, and 87 percent of risks), the highest loss per dollar of payroll, and higher claim frequency and severity in the voluntary market than in the residual market. This situation may partly reflect random noise, given the small exposure base in the voluntary market.

The difference between using unweighted and weighted means is evident from a comparison of the last two columns. Loss per $100 of payroll in both the residual and voluntary markets is two to three times higher using the unweighted mean than the more commonly cited weighted mean. This result suggests that, on average, smaller classes tend to have higher losses than larger classes; this finding, however, could also reflect higher variance and rightward skewness of the distribution of losses for small classes. Table 5–2 also reports the number of risks per $10,000 payroll, as a rough proxy for mean firm size.[13] This is at least two to three times higher in the residual market than in the voluntary market (except in Maine), suggesting that residual market risks are, on average, smaller firms.

---

13. The number of risks per $10,000 payroll is only an approximate indicator of firm size because risks includes only the firms for which this is the dominant class, whereas class payroll includes the payroll in this class for all firms in the market.

TABLE 5–2A
DIFFERENCES BETWEEN THE VOLUNTARY AND RESIDUAL MARKETS, 1988–1991
(unweighted means across classes)

State	Claims/Payroll ($10,000)		Loss/Claim		Risks/Payroll ($10,000)		Loss/Payroll ($100)(unweighted)		Loss/Payroll ($100)(weighed)	
	Voluntary	Residual	Voluntary	Residual	Voluntary	Residual	Voluntary	Residual	Voluntary	Residual
Michigan	0.118	0.199[a]	5,621.12	6,101.53[b]	0.042	0.100[a]	6.35	10.69[a]	2.24	4.92
Georgia	0.122	0.198[a]	3,986.73	5,204.67[a]	0.028	0.092[a]	5.05	10.47[a]	1.75	5.08
Illinois	0.091	0.141[a]	5,565.83	6,400.67[a]	0.027	0.078[a]	5.05	8.92[a]	1.53	3.23
Virginia	0.077	0.113[a]	4,548.51	7,857.24[a]	0.034	0.085[a]	3.62	9.07[a]	1.18	3.45
Alabama	0.110	0.183[a]	5,991.17	6,211.91	0.030	0.067[a]	6.19	11.10[a]	2.39	6.12
Florida	0.110	0.148[a]	9,295.16	15,351.53[a]	0.035	0.164[a]	10.51	22.60[a]	3.05	7.82
Louisiana	0.095	0.137[a]	7,073.18	7,372.03	0.033	0.086[a]	6.86	10.58[a]	2.25	4.57
Maine	0.233	0.145	8,775.35	9,465.53	0.054	0.065	16.70	13.48	4.84	6.07

a. Difference in means significant at $p = .01$.
b. Difference in means significant at $p = .05$.
SOURCE: Authors.

TABLE 5–2B
DIFFERENCES BETWEEN THE VOLUNTARY AND RESIDUAL MARKETS, 1985–1987
(unweighted means across classes)

State	Claims/Payroll ($10,000)		Loss/Claim		Risks/Payroll ($10,000)		Loss/Payroll ($100)(unweighted)		Loss/Payroll ($100)(weighted)	
	Voluntary	Residual	Voluntary	Residual	Voluntary	Residual	Voluntary	Residual	Voluntary	Residual
Michigan	0.124	0.209[a]	4,570.15	6,526.90[a]	0.046	0.103[a]	5.28	9.18[a]	1.90	4.43
Georgia	0.144	0.191[a]	2,827.44	4,138.51[a]	0.033	0.073[a]	4.08	8.07[a]	1.59	4.32
Illinois	0.105	0.146[a]	4,099.75	4,947.21[a]	0.030	0.076[a]	4.31	7.24[a]	1.32	2.68
Virginia	0.099	0.139[a]	3,637.04	4,848.82[a]	0.035	0.108[a]	3.67	6.36[a]	1.32	3.55
Alabama	0.129	0.195[a]	4,594.13	4,168.88	0.033	0.074[a]	5.91	7.73	2.15	5.48
Florida	0.128	0.164[a]	7,784.33	10,877.01[a]	0.038	0.146[a]	10.30	17.62[a]	3.32	7.47
Louisiana	0.112	0.145[a]	6,093.90	6,722.85	0.043	0.104[a]	7.13	10.13[a]	2.54	4.96
Maine	0.184	0.173	9,981.70	7,183.29[a]	0.048	0.072[a]	16.59	12.18[b]	7.23	6.20

a. Difference in means significant at $p = .01$.
b. Difference in means significant at $p = .05$.
SOURCE: Authors.

94

A comparison of table 5–2a and table 5–2b shows the change in mean claim costs by state over the period. Claim frequency has fallen in most states except Maine, whereas claim severity and total loss per exposure unit increased in all states (except in the voluntary market in Maine).

Table 5–3 reports mean growth rates over all classes in the seven states excluding Maine, for loss per $100 payroll, premium per $100 payroll, claim frequency, and claim severity. The standard deviations are often several times larger than the means because of the noise in the class-level data. The mean class growth in total loss per $100 of payroll between our two time periods was 16.9 percent, or roughly 7 percent a year, using the simple percentage growth rate. Growth was over twice as high in the residual market (37 percent) as in the voluntary market (15.2 percent). This growth in losses is driven primarily by the growth in claim severity, for which the marketwide average mean growth is 15.6 percent, composed of 33.9 percent for the residual market and 17.2 percent for the voluntary market.[14] Percentage growth in claim severity is higher in the residual market than in the voluntary market, which is consistent with the hypothesis that rate suppression, the lack of competition, and the pooling of losses result in more risky activity or less efficient claims management in the residual market. This ranking, however, is reversed using either absolute growth or log percentage growth.

Total claim frequency grew 2.7 percent. This figure reflects an increase of 8.5 percent for the residual market and only 0.7 percent in the voluntary market. By all three measures, the growth in claim frequency was more rapid in the residual market than in the voluntary market. This implies that any incentive for insurers to deny claims in response to rate suppression is more than offset by the

---

14. It is arithmetically possible for the mean for the total market to be less than the means for both of the two submarkets.

TABLE 5–3
COST GROWTH MEANS AND STANDARD DEVIATIONS
BY RESIDUAL, VOLUNTARY, AND TOTAL MARKETS

Variable	Market	Mean	STD
Absolute growth $(X_t - X_{t-1})$			
Loss/payroll	Total	0.007	0.027
	Residual	0.011	0.080
	Voluntary	0.004	0.030
Loss/claim (severity)	Total	0.535	2.279
	Residual	0.352	6.275
	Voluntary	0.468	2.583
Claims/payroll (frequency)	Total	0.049	2.155
	Residual	0.467	5.528
	Voluntary	0.197	2.393
Premium/payroll	Total	0.012	0.016
	Residual	0.015	0.021
	Voluntary	0.011	0.016
Percentage growth $(X_t / X_{t-1} - 1)$			
Loss/payroll	Total	0.169	0.378
	Residual	0.371	0.880
	Voluntary	0.152	0.425
Loss/claim (severity)	Total	0.156	0.367
	Residual	0.339	0.932
	Voluntary	0.172	0.439
Claims/payroll (frequency)	Total	0.027	0.211
	Residual	0.085	0.388
	Voluntary	0.007	0.244
Premium/payroll	Total	0.205	0.196
	Residual	0.234	0.237
	Voluntary	0.196	0.197
Log percentage growth (X_t / X_{t-1})			
Loss/payroll	Total	0.104	0.329
	Residual	0.100	0.720
	Voluntary	0.073	0.382

	TABLE 5–3 (continued)		
Variable	*Market*	*Mean*	*STD*
Loss/claim	Total	0.098	0.308
(severity)	Residual	0.075	0.697
	Voluntary	0.095	0.359
Claims/payroll	Total	0.006	0.201
(frequency)	Residual	0.025	0.340
	Voluntary	0.022	0.242
Premium/payroll	Total	0.173	0.016
	Residual	0.192	0.021
	Voluntary	0.166	0.016
Other			
Deficit/payroll $(t-1)$	Total	0.170	0.100
Benefit growth $(t-1)$	Total	1.021	0.133
Class residual market share $(t-1)$	Total	0.157	0.027
Residual market share growth	Total	0.033	0.072

Source: Authors.

claim-increasing effects of reduced incentives for loss control on the part of employers, employees, and insurers.

The mean increase in premium per $100 of payroll is 20.5 percent for the total market, composed of 23.4 percent in the residual market and 19.6 percent in the voluntary market. This compares with an increase in loss per $100 payroll of 37.1 percent for the residual market and 19.6 for the voluntary market. Thus, cross-subsidies from the voluntary market to the residual market appear to have increased over this period.

The mean residual market share of payroll is 20.4 percent including Maine, 15.7 percent excluding Maine. The growth in statewide residual market share is 4.1 percent including Maine and 3.3 percent excluding Maine. Including Maine doubles the estimate of residual market deficit per $100 statewide payroll, from $0.17 without Maine to $0.36 with Maine.

Absolute and percentage growth rates could be negatively correlated—for example, if classes with relatively low initial losses have higher percentage growth but lower absolute growth. In fact, the correlation between absolute growth and simple percentage growth in loss per $100 payroll is 0.73. Classes with a relatively high initial residual market share experienced more rapid growth in their residual market share ($r = 0.25$). Statutory benefit growth is negatively correlated with initial residual market share ($r = -0.13$).

Multivariate Analysis. Tables 5–4a and 5–4b report estimates of the effects of rate suppression on absolute and log percentage growth, respectively, in losses and premiums per $100 payroll. Three specifications are reported for each dependent variable. All include the lagged class-specific residual market share of payroll as a measure of rate suppression and industry dummy variables. Equation 1 includes state fixed effects (dummy variables) to control for unobserved state-specific influences on cost growth. Equations 2 and 3 replace the state fixed effects with substantive state variables: the lagged predicted growth in benefit costs for the state in both equations; the growth in the statewide mean residual market share in equation 2, to control for between-market selection effects; and the residual market deficit per $100 payroll in equation 3. The reduction in the adjusted R-squared indicates that the substantive state-level variables only partially control for all state-specific influences on cost growth that are reflected in the state fixed effects.

Total loss per $100 payroll. Table 5–4a confirms that absolute growth in loss per $100 payroll, by class, is positively related to rate suppression, measured by the class-specific lagged residual market share. The estimated effect is almost ten times greater in the residual market than in the voluntary market, where it is not significantly different from zero. Controlling for the growth in the statewide residual market share boosts the size and the significance of the estimated effect of lagged class-specific residual market share on loss growth in the residual market. The coefficient of the marketwide residual market share growth is not significant at the level of the aggregate market; it is, however, negative and significant for the residual and voluntary markets separately. These patterns are consistent with the hypothesis that residual market growth lowers the mean risk level in both the residual and voluntary submarkets because of selection effects, and hence leads to downward-biased estimates of their respective growth in costs.

The results for log percentage growth are similar. Thus, a high residual market share is associated with not only greater absolute cost growth but also greater percentage cost growth from an initially higher level.

States that enacted statutory benefit increases generally have more rapid growth in total loss per $100 payroll. This effect is greater for claim severity in the voluntary market but greater for claim frequency in the residual market. The insignificant effect in the residual market for total loss and for severity may simply reflect noise in the measure of losses for the residual market.

Claim severity. Absolute growth in claim severity is positively related to the class-specific residual market share. After controlling for the selection bias, the effect is statistically significant and greater for the residual market than for the voluntary market. This is as expected since the cost-increasing effects for the residual market include a greater employer moral hazard effect that increases high-risk activity (suppression of average rate levels and of ex-

TABLE 5–4A
EFFECT OF RATE SUPPRESSION ON ABSOLUTE COST GROWTH
(approximate absolute t-statistics using White standard errors in parentheses)

	Loss/Payroll			Loss/Claim			Claims/Payroll			Premium/Payroll		
	Total	Resid-ual	Volun-tary	Total	Resid-ual	Volun-tary	Total	Resid-ual	Volun-tary	Total	Resid-ual	Volun-tary
Equation 1[a]												
Class residual market share												
(t–1)	0.016	0.052	0.007	0.891	1.969	1.892	–0.373	3.623	–1.370	0.030	0.033	0.028
	(1.630)	(2.103)	(0.587)	(1.028)	(1.046)	(1.676)	(0.583)	(2.322)	(0.056)	(6.469)	(5.705)	(5.201)
Adjusted R^2	0.047	0.023	0.024	0.037	0.019	0.016	0.117	0.047	0.112	0.343	0.310	0.326
Equation 2[b]												
Class residual market share												
(t–1)	0.021	0.073	0.008	1.266	3.893	1.793	–0.424	2.483	–1.282	0.046	0.052	0.044
	(2.184)	(3.188)	(0.837)	(1.612)	(2.222)	(1.836)	(0.726)	(1.782)	(1.548)	(8.998)	(8.192)	(7.431)
Residual market share growth	–0.012	–0.096	–0.047	–3.000	–8.773	–3.026	3.356	–1.084	–0.130	–0.012	–0.041	–0.014
	(0.763)	(2.184)	(2.822)	(2.216)	(2.464)	(1.912)	(2.956)	(0.468)	(0.099)	(1.594)	(4.858)	(1.954)

Benefit growth (t−1)	0.044 (1.412)	0.000 (0.003)	0.050 (1.377)	3.617 (1.595)	−8.053 (0.998)	5.371 (2.106)	−3.700 (1.259)	29.956 (3.580)	−7.999 (2.554)	0.099 (6.247)	0.235 (8.836)	0.072 (4.827)
Adjusted R^2	0.037	0.021	0.020	0.034	0.013	0.018	0.063	0.024	0.066	0.236	0.231	0.214
Equation 3[b]												
Class residual market share (t−1)	0.016 (1.699)	0.059 (2.448)	0.006 (0.585)	1.052 (1.236)	2.572 (1.372)	2.046 (1.893)	−0.553 (0.847)	3.373 (2.174)	−1.632 (1.837)	0.031 (6.194)	0.037 (5.823)	0.028 (4.912)
Deficit/payroll (t−1)	0.005 (0.612)	−0.002 (0.065)	−0.010 (1.256)	−0.474 (0.696)	−0.054 (0.030)	−1.377 (1.784)	1.234 (2.129)	−2.024 (1.525)	0.631 (0.992)	0.027 (7.481)	0.016 (3.663)	0.026 (7.050)
Benefit growth (t−1)	0.043 (1.359)	−0.020 (0.170)	0.039 (1.074)	2.923 (1.294)	−9.931 (1.232)	4.569 (1.794)	−2.843 (0.976)	29.494 (3.553)	−7.955 (2.562)	0.100 (6.220)	0.228 (8.481)	0.072 (4.794)
Adjusted R^2	0.037	0.014	0.010	0.027	0.003	0.0160	0.058	0.027	0.067	0.281	0.222	0.257

a. Equation includes state and industry fixed effects.
b. Equation includes industry fixed effects.
SOURCE: Authors.

TABLE 5–4B

EFFECT OF RATE SUPPRESSION ON PERCENTAGE COST GROWTH

(approximate absolute t statistics using White standard errors in parentheses)

	Loss/Payroll			Loss/Claim			Claims/Payroll			Premium/Payroll		
	Total	Residual	Voluntary	Total	Residual	Voluntary	Total	Residual	Voluntary	Total	Residual	Voluntary
Equation 1[a]												
Class residual market share (t–1)	0.046 (0.427)	0.301 (1.448)	0.008 (0.064)	0.084 (0.752)	0.028 (0.140)	0.177 (1.252)	−0.037 (0.633)	0.273 (2.721)	−0.169 (1.763)	0.162 (3.659)	0.163 (3.294)	0.168 (3.081)
Adjusted R^2	0.045	0.010	0.058	0.029	0.005	0.033	0.128	0.045	0.118	0.346	0.321	0.318
Equation 2[b]												
Class residual market share (t–1)	0.065 (0.660)	0.436 (2.324)	0.016 (0.141)	0.090 (0.905)	0.202 (1.118)	0.156 (1.255)	−0.025 (0.468)	0.234 (2.673)	−0.139 (1.618)	0.391 (8.094)	0.418 (7.614)	0.391 (6.671)
Residual market share growth	−0.175 (1.020)	−0.575 (1.715)	−0.797 (3.883)	−0.417 (2.523)	−0.435 (1.371)	−0.591 (2.986)	0.243 (2.230)	−0.140 (0.830)	−0.206 (1.461)	0.091 (1.260)	−0.184 (2.270)	0.049 (0.647)

Benefit growth												
(t–1)	0.643	1.266	0.616	0.821	–0.179	1.046	–0.178	1.444	–0.430	1.766	2.643	1.480
	(1.565)	(1.358)	(1.358)	(2.099)	(0.194)	(2.449)	(0.726)	(3.162)	(1.583)	(9.303)	(10.711)	(7.618)
Adjusted R^2	0.019	0.005	0.035	0.022	0.001	0.025	0.060	0.022	0.061	0.173	0.177	0.147
Equation 3[b]												
Class residual market share												
(t–1)	0.077	0.390	0.045	0.128	0.121	0.232	–0.051	0.269	–0.187	0.185	0.227	0.186
	(0.711)	(1.905)	(0.350)	(1.158)	(0.621)	(1.704)	(0.862)	(2.746)	(1.958)	(4.024)	(4.232)	(3.256)
Deficit/payroll												
(t–1)	–0.073	–0.081	–0.290	–0.195	0.027	–0.320	0.122	–0.108	0.030	0.421	0.313	0.407
	(0.815)	(0.434)	(2.745)	(2.263)	(0.154)	(3.219)	(2.180)	(1.187)	(0.439)	(12.072)	(7.694)	(10.756)
Benefit growth												
(t–1)	0.597	1.134	0.413	0.709	–0.268	0.884	–0.112	1.402	–0.470	1.834	2.639	1.537
	(1.469)	(1.191)	(0.917)	(1.828)	(0.293)	(2.080)	(0.463)	(3.090)	(1.748)	(9.592)	(10.556)	(7.896)
Adjusted R^2	0.018	0.002	0.025	0.021	–0.001	0.026	0.059	0.023	0.058	0.288	0.216	0.254

a. Equation includes state and industry fixed effects.
b. Equation includes industry fixed effects.
SOURCE: Authors.

perience rating undermines employer incentives for loss control) and possibly suboptimal loss control due to the pooling of losses and lack of incentive to compete on service quality.

Any negative effect of loss pooling on insurer incentives for loss control would not affect the voluntary market. Thus, the positive association between rate suppression and claim severity growth in the voluntary market plausibly reflects weakened incentives of employer-employees for loss control due to attenuation of experience rating, which can coincide with suppression of average rate levels, or reduced insurer incentive due to constraints on insurer expense margins. It would be incorrect to assume that the difference between the residual and voluntary market effects is attributable solely to the pooling of residual market losses, because the employer moral hazard effect also is expected to be greater in the residual market than in the voluntary market.

It might be argued that the higher growth in claim severity in the residual market could simply reflect the fact that residual markets include a disproportionate number of small firms for which insurer and employer loss-control incentives are weak because small firms are not experience-rated. While our data on the number of risks per $100 of payroll could indicate relatively more small firms in the residual market if only a small firm effect were operating, cost growth would be higher in the residual market but not necessarily positively related to residual market size at the class code level.

The log percentage growth rate for claim severity is positively related to residual market share, but this effect is not significant at conventional levels. Taken at face value, this indicates that although residual market share has a positive effect on absolute cost growth, this effect is not sufficiently large to compensate for the higher base level and to generate a positive percentage effect. In general, explanatory power as measured by adjusted R-squared is lower for the log percentage growth rate than for absolute cost growth.

Claim frequency. Growth in claim frequency in the residual market is significantly positively related to the lagged residual market share, consistent with the hypothesis that rate suppression increases the frequency of injuries or claims or both. For the voluntary market, the estimated effect is negative but only marginally significant. These two effects cancel out such that there is no significant effect on claim frequency at the marketwide level. These conclusions hold for both absolute growth and for log percentage growth.

Recall from chapter 3 that the effect of residual market share on claim frequency is theoretically ambiguous. This finding of a positive effect in the residual market but a negative effect in the voluntary market is consistent with the hypothesis that in the residual market the positive effect of higher risk activity and possibly reduced investments in insurer loss control dominates any negative service quality effect that could be associated with higher claim rejection rates and hence lower reported frequency, as well as any positive effect of implicit taxes in voluntary market premiums on safety for firms in the voluntary market.

Growth in claim frequency is higher in states in which the state mean residual market share increased over our period, although the relationship is negative but insignificant for the voluntary and residual markets separately (which might be affected by possibly lower precision of estimation with disaggregated data). The positive effect at the classwide level is consistent with selection bias due to increased self-insurance; it could also reflect, however, other omitted variables that are correlated with residual market share growth.

Growth in statutory benefits is positively related to claim frequency growth in the residual market but negatively related to frequency growth in the voluntary market.

These offsetting effects result in an insignificant negative positive effect for the total market.

Premium growth. Growth in manual premium per $100 payroll is significantly positively related to residual market share for the total market and for the voluntary and residual submarkets separately. This confirms our basic hypothesis that rate suppression is counterproductive: by increasing cost growth, rate suppression ultimately leads to higher premiums. The similar coefficients for the voluntary and residual markets confirm that residual market deficits are shifted in part to voluntary market risks within the same state. The fact that loss per $100 payroll for the voluntary market is not significantly related to residual market share (the positive effect on severity is offset by a negative effect on frequency) suggests that this positive effect of residual market share on voluntary market premiums primarily reflects cost shifting from the residual market, rather than cost growth in the voluntary market itself.

Premium growth is also significantly and positively related to lagged statutory benefit growth. The coefficients for percentage growth are significantly greater than one and greater in the residual market than in the voluntary market, although coefficients for losses are less than one in all three markets. The larger coefficients in the premium equations could reflect a lag in adjusting premiums; they could also reflect other unobservable state characteristics that are correlated with lagged benefit growth.

The residual market deficit per $100 payroll was expected to be positively related to cost growth in the residual market under the increasing returns to scale hypothesis (residual market carriers adjust their behavior more, the larger the size of the residual market deficit). Contrary to this prediction, this variable is generally either negative or insignificant in the residual market equations for cost growth. It is, however, significantly and positively related to premium growth per $100 payroll, with a greater effect in the voluntary market than in the residual market. This result further confirms that some fraction of residual market deficits is passed through to other policyholders in the same state. We return to this issue of cross-subsidies in chapter 6.

Conclusions

This evidence from class-level data confirms the findings reported in chapter 4 using state-level data: rate suppression exacerbates cost growth and hence ultimately leads to higher premiums, contrary to its initial intent. The cost-increasing effects are greater in the residual market than in the voluntary market. Compared with the cost-increasing effects, however, the premium-increasing effects appear to be greater in the voluntary market because of cost shifting.

Larger cost-increasing effects of rate suppression in the residual market than in the voluntary market are consistent with the hypothesis of greater employer moral hazard effects in the residual market, due to greater suppression of aggregate rate levels and the attenuation of experience rating. This effect may be exacerbated if insurer incentives for loss control are weaker in the residual market. Unfortunately, the data available are insufficient to determine the relative contribution of these different factors. Finding a positive effect of residual market share on claim severity in the voluntary market is most plausibly explained by possible attenuation of experience rating for some firms (and by reduced investment in loss control). The lack of a positive relation between cost growth and the statewide residual market deficit is inconsistent with the joint hypothesis that pooling reduces insurer incentives for loss control and that the effect becomes greater as the total size of the residual market and deficit increase.

6
Cross-Subsidy Effects
of Rate Regulation

The stated objective of rate regulation is to ensure that rates are not excessive, inadequate, or unfairly discriminatory. While some disagreement about appropriate rates no doubt reflects differences in judgment about trends in loss costs, the cost of capital, etc., the inherent uncertainty can be exploited by the political process. Rate regulation, like other forms of government intervention, creates an opportunity for politically powerful groups to intervene to obtain cross-subsidies through rates that differ systematically from expected costs, conditional on available information.[1]

This chapter analyzes the extent of systematic cross-subsidies in workers' compensation insurance and tests simple hypotheses derived from economic models of political pressure. Understanding the nature of systematic cross-subsidies in rate regulation is useful in evaluating their distributive effects. It also provides supporting evidence relevant to the allocative effects documented in chapters 4 and 5, since persistent rate suppression to particular classes is a prerequisite for the behavioral responses that lead to excessive cost growth.

---

1. The economic theory of political decision making is developed in Stigler (1971), Peltzman (1976), and Becker (1983). For application of these models to automobile insurance, see Harrington (1992) and Harrington and Doerpinghaus (1993); for workers' compensation benefit structures see Danzon (1987).

Previous studies of rate regulation in automobile and workers' compensation insurance have examined effects of regulatory structure—prior approval or open competition (often broadly defined)—on statewide average rate levels to test hypotheses of industry versus consumer capture of the regulatory process.[2] The evidence suggests that rate regulation in recent years has benefited consumers rather than insurers but that specific forms of regulation can have different effects in different states. Klein, Nordman, and Fritz (1993), for example, find that the mean loss ratio for workers' compensation is not significantly different between states with traditional prior approval and states with less restrictive regulation. This evidence suggests that broad regulatory structure may be a misleading indicator of distributive effects and that the devil is in the details of implementation. Here we go beneath the broad regulatory structure and the statewide average rate level to examine rate suppression and cross-subsidies at the level of the individual rating class.

A Simple Theory of Cross-Subsidies

The Incidence of Cross-Subsidies. Economic theory and empirical evidence conclude that the long-run incidence of workers' compensation premium costs is largely on workers through compensating wage offsets.[3] Thus, the primary

---

2. For a summary of the literature on automobile regulation, see Harrington (1984). Klein, Nordman, and Fritz (1993) document the association between rate regulation and growth in residual markets in workers' compensation. Chelius and Smith (1987) report differences in loss ratios by firm size. Their evidence suggests that rate setting in workers' compensation favors small firms but that this is offset by higher administrative costs due to diseconomies of small scale. Also see Harrington (1988b).

3. For evidence of the incidence of workers' compensation costs, see Viscusi and Moore (1987), Moore and Viscusi (1990), and Gruber and Krueger (1990).

beneficiaries of rate suppression are workers for whom rates are suppressed below competitive levels, who benefit from higher wages or more jobs than would be available if insurers charged actuarial rates. Some costs, however, may fall on owners of immobile factors such as entrepreneurial capital because of such factors as short-run deviations in insurance rates from levels that are anticipated in wage contracts or from levels that prevail for similar employees in other states.[4]

The *net* gain to beneficiaries of rate suppression may be less than implied by the *gross* reduction in premiums because of cost increases and reduction in service quality, as described above. We assume that any reduction in the real value of benefits does not fully offset the reduction in premiums, such that premium-based measures of rate suppression remain valid indicators of directions of cross-subsidies, although magnitudes may be overstated.[5]

The incidence of the costs of rate suppression may differ across states, depending on the magnitude of the deficit, the industrial structure, and details of regulation. In principle, unless prevented by regulation, insurers might be able to recover the ex ante cost of expected residual market deficits incurred from writing business in a given year by charging higher premiums in the voluntary market, in which case rate suppression would operate as a pure system of taxes and subsidies between policyholders in a

---

4. Danzon (1988, 1989) uses a general equilibrium model to show that the incidence of state-mandated workers' compensation or health insurance may be partly based on immobile factors, such as entrepreneurial capital in small firms.

5. If there were not a net gain at least in the short run, investing in political influence would be irrational. Moreover, the evidence in chapter 5 on differences in loss ratios and the discrepancy between premium growth and cost growth across classes and between states strongly suggests that net cross-subsidies are realized. Ideally, we would like to test the impact of cross-subsidies on wage rates, but class-level data on wage rates are not available.

state (see chapter 2). In practice, the extent of the pass-through of actual and expected deficits to voluntary market rates may be constrained for several reasons. If, for example, the deficit for prior years' business unexpectedly increases and the increase in assessments is viewed as a sunk cost by insurers, there would be no pass-through of the increase, assuming that voluntary market rates are already at profit-maximizing levels.[6] If regulation constrains voluntary market rates below profit-maximizing levels, however, and if this constraint is relaxed by the regulatory authorization to pass through increased residual market losses, then unexpected increases in residual market losses might be shifted to policyholders in the voluntary market.

Even if residual market deficits are persistent, such that insurers perceive expected future residual market assessments as an ad valorem tax on writing new business in the voluntary market, short-run increases in the estimated cost of residual market deficits may not be fully passed on to policyholders in the voluntary market, depending on the elasticity of demand in the voluntary market. The option for employers to self-insure, for example, may limit the pass-through of increases in the expected residual market deficit to the voluntary market in the short run. Self-insured employers avoid all cross-subsidies implicit in the regulated premium structure and assessments for residual market deficits. Some firms, however, face significant obstacles to

---

6. An insurer that is already charging the profit-maximizing premium to a particular risk has no incentive to change that rate just because of a retroactive charge based on past business—indeed, to do so would reduce expected profits. An exception might occur in the event of large unexpected increases in prior years' deficits that could reduce insurer capital and cause a backward shift in short-run supply. In this case, switching costs for employers and insurers' sunk investments in acquiring information about specific employers' risk characteristics may allow the employer's current insurer some margin to recoup residual market assessments from prior years, even if other insurers in the market could charge lower rates due to lower assessments.

self-insurance due to regulatory restrictions and to small size and related costs.

Moreover, severe suppression of residual market rates not only increases the residual market deficit but may also limit the pass-through of that deficit to policyholders in the voluntary market because residual market rates act as a ceiling on voluntary market rates. Thus, heavy suppression of residual market rates both increases the deficit per policy in the residual market and reduces the rates that can be charged in the voluntary market; this reduces the proportion of policies that can be written in the voluntary market, thereby shrinking the "tax" base against which the (larger) expected residual market deficit can be charged.

To the extent that the pass-through of residual market deficits to voluntary market premiums is limited by either regulation of voluntary market rates or competition among insurers and policyholders shifting to self-insurance, part of the cost of residual market deficits falls on insurance equity.[7] In the short run, insurers may be willing to incur some losses on fully allocated costs as long as rates cover marginal costs, because exit entails the loss of quasi-rents on sunk investments (see Harrington 1992).[8] Here we focus on within-state cross-subsidies between workers' compensation policyholders. A more complex model and more comprehensive data would be required to analyze the possible shifting of net losses to other insurance lines, states, or insurer equity.

---

7. Shifting losses to other lines or other states is inconsistent with profit maximization under normal assumptions about cost and demand structures.

8. Legal restrictions on exit from the workers' compensation market are generally limited to requirements for sufficient notice of policy cancellations and nonrenewal (Klein, Nordman, and Fritz 1993). Consistent with the hypothesis that insurer capital is imperfectly mobile, Kramer (1992) reports that companies whose business is concentrated in states with significant rate suppression for auto or workers' compensation have lower total return on net worth (book value).

Interest groups may seek to obtain cross-subsidies by influencing several dimensions of rate regulation. By influencing the manual rates for the voluntary and residual markets and rate relativities between classes, transfers can be enforced from low to high risks within each class and between classes. Cross-subsidies from low to high risks within a class can also result from regulatory constraints on experience rating, on ex post dividends, and on other adjustments that reward policyholders for good loss experience. The experience-rating formula is designed such that the ratio of standard (after experience rating) to manual premiums averages out to one across classes within each state. Thus, restrictions on experience rating imply a within-state system of subsidies from low to high risks. Although some policyholders may gain, in general it is a negative sum game because of the adverse effects of rate suppression on cost growth, as shown. Restrictions on self-insurance also facilitate cross-subsidies from low to high risks.

Our data on manual and standard premiums for each class do not reflect dividends, schedule credits, and other adjustments.[9] Since these rating adjustments are used to reward low risks and penalize high risks, our data on manual and standard premium rates probably understate the true degree of dispersion in premiums and thus overestimate the subsidies to high risks and the implicit "taxes" paid by good risks. Our data should, however, provide reliable evidence on the direction of cross-subsidies.

Moreover, manual and standard premiums should be a reasonably accurate indicator of actual premiums and

9. Manual premiums reflect the product of class rates (from the rating manual) and the appropriate exposure base (generally payroll). Standard premiums equal manual premiums adjusted for experience-rating modifications. Actual transactions rates may also differ from these listed rates because of schedule rating and the extent that employers, agents, and insurers manipulate payroll classification to manipulate price.

cross-subsidies in states that severely restrict insurer deviations; these are the states where investments in political influence are likely to be greatest. In states that permit individual insurers broad flexibility to deviate from manual rates, interest groups have less incentive to attempt to influence voluntary market manual rates, since these rates are not a binding constraint on rates actually charged by insurers. Conversely, incentives to influence manual rates are greatest where this flexibility for adjustments to manual rates is most constrained. Even in moderately regulated states, manual rates may accurately indicate rate relativities across classes if insurer deviations take the form of fixed percentage deviations from manual rates.

General Principles of Political Influence. The theory of political influence assumes that potential interest groups make rational investments in political pressure, weighing the expected gain from investing in influence against the costs. Politicians and regulators are assumed to act as rational intermediaries, responding to political influence in the form of money and votes.

In general, the political power of a group is positively related to the number of votes and dollar resources that it can bring to bear, which depend on the total stakes or value of the potential subsidy to the group, net of the costs of organization. Larger groups generally have higher stakes and greater voting power, other things being equal. Offsetting this advantage of size is the requirement of subsidies to larger groups for greater taxes on other groups—either higher tax rates or a broader tax base.

Given the total potential stakes for a group, its effective power is likely to be greater, the more concentrated the benefits and the smaller the number of stakeholders. This assumes that becoming informed and organizing to exert pressure entail a fixed cost per firm, such that costs of organization are larger, relative to expected benefits, the greater the number of stakeholders in the group. A group with a larger number of stakeholders also faces higher free-rider incentives. Conversely, it may command more votes.

These general principles suggest certain hypotheses about the characteristics of classes that are likely to be winners and losers from workers' compensation rate regulation. Potentially important characteristics include relative payroll, high risks, low-wage workers, concentrated versus diffused classes, and concentration across states.

Relative payroll. The greater the payroll of the class$_i$ relative to the mean payroll per class for the state (payroll$_i$/payroll $(t-1)$), the greater the proportion of employees affected and the greater the stakes per employee—hence the greater the incentive for investment in influence and the proportion of votes that the class represents. A subsidy of 20 percent for a class that accounts for 10 percent of state payroll, however, requires higher taxes on other stakeholders than for a class that represents only 0.1 percent of state payroll. The implication is that relatively large classes may be subsidized but, in any case, are unlikely to be severely taxed. We use a lagged measure of relative payroll and other explanatory variables under the assumption that the rate structure in period *t* reflects influence in the prior period. Since our analysis includes a proxy control for low wages per employee (see below), a relatively high payroll primarily indicates a class with a relatively large number of employees, not high wages per employee.

High risks. Classes with a high pure premium per dollar of payroll have greater impact on an employer's overall premium cost, *ceteris paribus*. The potential gain from a given percentage suppression of rates is therefore greater, the higher the pure premium (loss) per dollar of payroll. Equity norms may also favor cross-subsidies to occupations with high premiums relative to payroll, which would lower the opposition to rate suppression for these classes and

115

increase the payoff to investments in influence. There may also be efficiency gains from subsidies to high-risk firms. Many of these are small firms for which coverage is optional. Subsidies increasing the proportion of such firms that purchase coverage would reduce the negative externalities that may result if uninsured losses are cost-shifted to other firms in the state.[10] As measures of high risk, we include claim frequency (claims per $100 payroll) and claim severity (loss per claim). The natural log transform is used to reduce the influence of outlier values.

Low-wage workers. Actuarially fair premiums are likely to be a larger fraction of payroll for low-wage occupations for several reasons. Unskilled jobs may entail greater intrinsic risk of compensable injury. Less-skilled workers may also be less skilled at avoiding accidents and hence incur a higher frequency of accidents. The structure of workers' compensation benefits provides a higher replacement rate of indemnity loss for low-wage workers;[11] in addition, if medical loss per claim is less than proportionately higher for high-wage workers, medical loss is a higher proportion for low-wage workers.[12] Moreover, since residual market "taxes" are proportional to premiums, the tax rate per dol-

---

10. For a similar analysis applied to high-risk drivers, who are major beneficiaries from rate regulation in automobile insurance, see Harrington (1988a).

11. Indemnity payments are proportional to wage level up to the maximum weekly benefit, such that indemnity payments decline as a proportion of wages at a higher wage level.

12. Although the income elasticity of demand for medical care is positive in broad cross-sections and in time series, this does not necessarily apply to postinjury use of medical services. Moreover, because workers' compensation has low, if any, copayments and these are uniform across income levels, the insurance-induced positive correlation between income and medical care use that is observed in health insurance data (wealthier families buy more coverage and hence face lower point-of-service prices) does not apply to medical expense covered by workers' compensation.

lar of payroll and per employee is a higher percentage on classes with high premium rates per dollar of payroll. Since these high-cost classes are also typically high-risk or low-wage occupations, the inequity of the residual market tax system may be another reason favoring cross-subsidies to low-wage classes through the class relativities.

Assuming that low-wage workers would face higher premium rates per dollar of payroll, they have greater incentives to invest in political influence, and this tendency may be consistent with social goals of redistribution. We do not have class-level data on wages per employee. Because premium per dollar of payroll is expected to be positively correlated with low wages, however, these considerations related to low-wage effects lead to the prediction that rate suppression benefits classes with high expected loss per dollar of payroll. Expected loss is measured here decomposed into claim frequency and claim severity. Unfortunately, this prediction regarding effects of low wages is empirically indistinguishable from the previous prediction, that rate suppression favors high-risk jobs.

Concentrated versus diffuse classes. The expected return to employers from investment in influencing rates is greater for classes that account for a relatively large share of payroll and premium. Moreover, free-rider effects may operate such that, controlling for relative payroll, classes that are relatively concentrated are more likely to benefit from rate suppression than classes that are dispersed over a large number of employers. The database reports for each class the number of employers for which that class is the dominant class (risks) and the total number of employers that employ that class (class count). Classes that are employed by a relatively large number of employers (class count$_i$ divided by the mean value of the class count) may be subject to free-rider effects that are expected to reduce the ability to obtain subsidies. Classes that have a relatively large number of risks, relative to the mean number of risks per class

117

in the state (risk$_i$ divided by the mean value of risks) are the dominant class for a relatively large number of firms and hence might be expected to benefit from rate suppression. Controlling for relative payroll, however, a high value of relative risks could reflect predominantly small firms. We return to this below.

In practice, distinguishing separate effects of relative payroll size, relative number of risks, and class count is problematic because these measures are highly correlated. The correlation between relative risks and class count is .76; between relative risks and payroll is .67; and between relative class count and payroll is .96 (data for seven states).

Employer size. Large firms face lower costs and risks of self-insuring than do smaller firms, because of regulatory constraints on self-insurance by small firms and the advantages of size in spreading fixed costs and bearing risk. Large firms are, therefore, less likely to be taxed, other things equal.

Small firm size, however, is likely to be correlated with in-state ownership of a high proportion of capital, which may be associated with high stakes and low costs of exerting influence. If the full incidence of costs and benefits is on workers, all of whom are in-state residents, then the benefits and costs of exerting pressure should not differ between domestically owned firms and firms owned by out-of-state corporations. But if workers' compensation costs are borne partly by entrepreneurial capital or other immobile firm-specific factors, then domestic firms may be more successful at exerting political pressure than out-of-state firms. Domestic firms may have higher stakes due to local investments in immobile capital, and lower costs, better information, greater voting power, and indirect local influence.

Conversely, state-specific sunk investments are vulnerable to appropriation of quasi-rents, for employers as for insurers. Such vulnerability could make in-state employer capital vulnerable to regulatory "taxes." Thus, assuming that state-specific investments are lower for firms with out-of-state ownership, out-of-state employers are unlikely to be heavily taxed because they can make a credible threat to move out of state. If out-of-state firms are also generally larger, this factor reinforces the prediction that large firms are unlikely to be heavily taxed.

The predictions with respect to the net effects of employer size are thus ambiguous. Small firms are likely to gain from rate suppression if there are positive net benefits from in-state ownership that outweigh the disadvantages of small size for self-insurance.[13]

Concentration across states. Occupations that are employed in many states are likely to be relatively mobile, in which case they cannot be heavily taxed in individual states. Less diffuse classes may be less mobile; since they are relatively concentrated in a few states, however, they have greater stakes per state so have greater payoff to investment in obtaining rate suppression in those states. We use a Herfindahl index of the concentration of each class across the twenty-seven states in our database to test whether rate suppression is systematically related to concentration.[14]

Alternative Models of Cross-Subsidies. There are at least three possible patterns of cross-subsidies: aggregate state-wide rate inadequacy, with losses borne by insurer equity

---

13. The hypotheses related to size pertain to the size of the employer, not the insurer. The size distribution of insurers would also be relevant for an analysis of cross-subsidies from insurer equity, but this is not our focus here.

14. The Herfindahl index for each class is the sum of the squared shares of countrywide payroll in each state in which that class is present. It ranges from 1 for a class that is concentrated in a single state to 0.034 for a highly diffuse class. The mean is 0.0586, indicating that most classes are relatively diffuse across the states in which the class is present. States in which a class is not present are excluded from the measure.

(or, much less plausibly, by policyholders in other lines or states); between-class cross-subsidies within a state; and within-class cross-subsidies within a class and a state. These transfers are not mutually exclusive. If rates are inadequate statewide for all classes with no pass-through of residual market losses to the voluntary market, for example, then there is a subsidy to all classes, but there are neither between-class nor within-class cross-subsidies in a state. Alternatively, between-class and within-class cross-subsidies could be fully offsetting, such that rates for the state as a whole are adequate. A third possibility—and probably the norm— is a combination of all three types of transfers. In general, if some employers in a class are in the residual market while other employers in that class are insured in the voluntary market and pay a price that includes a surcharge to subsidize the residual market, the result might be viewed as a within-class cross-subsidy, since some employers within the class are taxed while others are subsidized. Even if voluntary market prices do not increase to fund expected residual market deficits, residual market rate suppression will cause relative price-cost margins to differ for the voluntary and residual markets within a class.

The different forms of cross-subsidies would result from different patterns of political influence and imply different allocative effects of rate suppression. In particular, within-class cross-subsidies favor high-risk firms at the expense of low-risk firms within specific industries. Such within-class subsidies are likely to encourage an excessive number of high-risk firms within each industry, but the industrial mix is not necessarily affected. By contrast, between-class cross-subsidies may distort the industrial mixture, but the competitive positions of different firms within an industry are not necessarily affected.

The analysis here focuses on between-class and within-class cross-subsidies. We also provide evidence on aggregate statewide rate suppression. A detailed analysis, however, would require a more extensive model and data including other interest groups, which is beyond the scope of this study.[15]

Data and Methodology

Our analysis of within-class subsidies uses class-level data on the leading 150 classes in seven states (Alabama, Florida, Maine, Louisiana, Virginia, Georgia, and Michigan) for which residual and voluntary market data are reported separately.[16] For some tests for between-class subsidies, we use marketwide data for all classes in twenty-seven states.[17] These data are for five policy years spanning December 1985–January 1992. The total number of classes in a state ranges from 171 to 510, reflecting differences in the industrial mix. The data reported for each class reflect the experience of all insurers and all insured employers within that class. As noted, these data do not report the experience of individual employers within a class or actual premiums charged by individual insurers.

To control for the long payout tail and to put all policy years on a more consistent basis, we develop reported loss costs and claim frequency to expected ultimate maturity, using the NCCI's state-specific development factors for medical loss, indemnity loss, and claim frequency. We adjust all dollar values to constant 1992 dollars, using a wage index for payroll and indemnity loss, the medical component of the CPI for medical loss, and a weighted average of the medical and wage indexes for premiums.

The class-level data are highly unstable across years, particularly for losses. To average out some of the stochas-

---

15. A model of statewide rate inadequacy should consider other likely beneficiary groups, including attorneys and some medical providers. Detailed data on length of the payout tail and direct writer share (to control for expenses) would also be necessary.

16. Illinois could not be included because of missing data for some variables.

17. The NCCI maintains data at the class code level for these states.

tic variation, we use two- and three-year mean values, as was done in the analysis of cost growth at the class code level.[18] To reduce the influence of extreme values further, for the analysis of loss ratios we use the log transformation and eliminate outliers, defined as observations that are more than four standard deviations from the mean. Classes with missing data on key variables are omitted.

A White test indicates significant heteroscedasticity for some OLS regressions, even using three-year means. We report approximate *t*-statistics using White standard errors. Preliminary analysis showed little, if any, efficiency gain from using weighted least squares, with weights defined as the predicted value from a regression of OLS squared residuals on the inverse of payroll and number of risks.

Empirical Results

Evidence of Persistent Cross-Subsidies. The most basic hypothesis of political influence is that patterns of rate suppression are persistent over time in specific states and classes. The null hypothesis is that differences in loss ratios between states and classes are random, resulting from stochastic shocks that average out over time.

By state. Tables 5–1 and 5–2 report the residual market share of payroll, risks and premiums, loss ratios, and the ratio of filed to approved rates for the residual market, the voluntary market, and the weighted average for the eight states where residual market data are available by class. The significant differences in these measures across states and the persistence of these patterns across the five years support the hypothesis of persistent statewide rate suppression in some states compared with other states.

---

18. The three-year mean loss ratio is the sum of losses divided by the sum of premiums.

By class. If an increase in rate suppression statewide entails increased cross-subsidies between classes within the state, then states with relatively high mean loss ratios should have greater dispersion in loss ratios between classes, reflecting the use of excessive premiums (relative to losses) for taxed classes to subsidize inadequate premiums for other classes. If a higher mean loss ratio for a state generally is not associated with greater between-class dispersion in loss ratios, the increase in subsidies to some classes must be borne fully by insurer equity (or, again less plausibly, by policyholders in other lines or states).

We identified states in the top and bottom quartiles, respectively, of the distribution of state mean loss ratios in the earliest two policy years (period B) and in the most recent three policy years (period A). For each of these states, we estimate the distribution of loss ratios across classes. The hypothesis of increased between-class cross subsidies predicts that the interquartile range of the distribution of class-specific loss ratios should be higher for states with high mean loss ratios than for states with low mean loss ratios.

The evidence confirms that an increase in the mean statewide loss ratio is associated with an increase in the interquartile range. For states in quartile 4 in period A, the interquartile range across classes ranges from 2.4 to 5.7, with a median of .90. For states in quartile 1 in period A, the range is from 1.7 to 4.0, with a median of .60. A similar pattern appears in period B. This evidence supports the hypothesis that at least some of the deficit increase associated with increased statewide mean rate suppression is borne by taxed classes in the same state.

By industry. To test the hypothesis that statewide rate suppression effects cross-subsidies between industries within a state, we performed a similar analysis at the level of the industry. If firms in the same industry have common class structures and lower costs of coordinating lobbying efforts, for example, through use of industrywide union and employer organizations, then cross-subsidies should follow industry lines. The alternative hypothesis is that industry-wide lobbying is undermined by either differences in the class mix across firms in an industry or other obstacles to cooperation.

We find little evidence that cross-subsidies follow industry lines, at least using the NCCI definition of industries, which corresponds roughly but not exactly to the standard industrial classification (SIC). There is weak evidence in the early period that the interquartile range across industries is higher in states with a high mean loss ratio, but no such pattern appears in the later period. Consistent with this, we find no evidence of strong industry effects in the multivariate analysis described below.

Between-Class Cross-Subsidies. The economic model of political influence predicts that rate regulation will be used to effect cross-subsidies between classes within a state. Since the occupational mix and the industry structure differ across states, a specific class could be relatively influential and hence a net winner in one state but a net loser in another state in which it has less influence relative to other classes. Thus, the characteristics that convey relative power (for example, relative payroll size, mean firm size, concentration) could be the same across states, although the identity of beneficiary classes could differ across states. Alternatively, certain classes could be systematic winners or losers across states because of industry-related factors that convey relative political influence in most states, such as unionization. We test for industry-specific effects across states by including a vector of industry dummy variables in some equations. These hypotheses are tested using residual market share and loss ratios as alternative measures of mean class gain from rate regulation.

Residual market shares by class. Between-class cross-subsidies should cause differences in the residual market share across classes.[19] The percentage of class payroll in the residual market is a rough measure of the percentage of employees who pay subsidized rates as a result of rate suppression; the residual market share of risks is the percentage of employers that pay subsidized rates among employers for which this class is the dominant class.

Table 6–1 reports equations for the residual market share of payroll and the share of risks, by class, for the top 150 classes in seven states.[20] The dependent variable is the log odds ratio of the average residual market share over the three most recent years.[21] For explanatory variables that are potentially endogenous, we use a lagged value, defined as the mean for the prior two years. Three equations are reported for each dependent variable. The first includes the class-specific measures of influence and three state-specific variables that do not differ across classes in a state. The ratio of filed to approved rates controls for differences across states in the mean level of rate suppression. The estimated effect of statutory benefit change on loss costs, for the current and lagged periods, is included to control for possible lags in adjusting premiums to reflect benefit changes. The second equation replaces these substantive state variables with a vector of state fixed effects. The third equation adds a vector of industry fixed effects and relative class count.

For the residual market share of payroll, most indicators of political influence are significant, with signs that are consistent with the theory of political influence. Subsidies are significantly positively related to claim frequency per \$100 of payroll and to claim severity ($\text{loss}_i/\text{claim}_i$). This is consistent with the hypothesis that classes with relatively

19. Some differences in residual market share across classes might arise even if all cross-subsidies are within one class.

20. Illinois is omitted because data on class count are not reported.

21. Results were similar using the residual market share as the dependent variable. The log odds transformation ensures that predicted values, when retransformed, are nonnegative.

TABLE 6–1
RESIDUAL MARKET SHARE, BY CLASS, THREE-YEAR MEANS, IN SEVEN STATES
(absolute *t*-statistics using White standard errors in parentheses)

Variable	Share of Payroll			Share of Risks		
	Equation 1	Equation 2	Equation 3	Equation 1	Equation 2	Equation 3
Intercept	133.552	3.855	4.505	89.005	0.586	0.853
	(11.525)	(7.967)	(8.185)	(8.903)	(1.559)	(2.022)
Log (loss per claim$_i$)(t–1)	0.381	0.121	0.191	0.715	0.347	0.339
	(5.604)	(1.856)	(2.428)	(11.663)	(6.581)	(5.613)
Log (claim frequency$_i$)(t–1)	0.347	0.205	0.337	0.327	0.204	0.282
	(5.381)	(3.621)	(4.805)	(6.345)	(5.299)	(5.775)
Risks$_i$ / $\overline{\text{risks}}$ (t–1)	0.010	–0.018	0.017	–0.040	–0.065	–0.045
	(0.486)	(1.078)	(1.017)	(1.939)	(4.127)	(3.012)
Payroll$_i$/ $\overline{\text{payroll}}$ (t–1)	0.014	0.012	0.112	0.020	0.018	0.062
	(1.742)	(2.015)	(4.979)	(2.624)	(3.405)	(2.840)
Log (payroll$_i$/ class count$_i$) (t–1)	–0.474	–0.519	–0.593	–0.137	–0.183	–0.185
	(11.748)	(13.494)	(11.473)	(4.454)	(7.114)	(5.585)
Class count$_i$/ $\overline{\text{class count}}$ (t–1)	—	—	–0.154	—	—	–0.071
	—	—	(5.568)	—	—	(2.662)

	(1)	(2)	(3)	(4)	(5)	(6)
Statutory benefit growth $(t-1)$	-80.333 (24.425)	—	—	-62.171 (23.394)	—	—
Filed/approved $(t-1)$	9.957 (26.755)	—	—	7.893 (26.248)	—	—
Statutory benefit growth (t)	-60.089 (6.532)	—	—	-35.635 (4.461)	—	—
Alabama	—	0.545 (4.274)	0.478 (4.004)	—	0.429 (4.045)	0.431 (4.481)
Florida	—	0.043 (0.369)	-0.107 (0.875)	—	0.553 (5.309)	0.497 (4.953)
Georgia	—	-0.286 (2.340)	-0.333 (2.802)	—	-0.211 (2.130)	-0.201 (2.195)
Louisiana	—	1.564 (11.702)	1.480 (10.942)	—	1.433 (13.123)	1.420 (13.589)
Maine	—	3.641 (24.494)	3.485 (22.517)	—	2.948 (28.332)	2.941 (28.507)
Michigan	—	-1.213 (10.108)	-1.329 (11.274)	—	-1.473 (15.378)	-1.468 (16.184)
Adjusted R^2	0.639	0.711	0.745	0.603	0.743	0.779

NOTE: Subscript i denotes class level variable. Overstrike denotes a mean access class.
Dependent variable $= \log [s_i / (1-s_i)]$
SOURCE: Authors.

high premium costs relative to payroll, due to either high-risk activities or low wages, have greater incentives to exert pressure for subsidies and face less resistance to subsidies. Classes that have a large payroll, relative to mean class payroll in a state (payroll$_i$ divided by the mean value of the payroll dollar) have higher residual market shares, as expected if the number of employees enhances political influence. The evidence on the effects of concentrated versus diffuse classes is mixed. The significant negative coefficient on relatively diffuse classes (class count$_i$ divided by the mean value of the class count) supports the hypothesis that diffuse classes are politically weak because of the low stakes per firm and free-rider problems. The insignificant coefficient on relative number of risks (risks$_i$ divided by the mean value of risks), however, is inconsistent with the hypothesis that employers have higher stakes in influencing rates for dominant classes. In general, conclusions on the effects of concentration are tentative because of the high correlation between these variables and relative payroll size.

The residual market share is negatively related to mean firm size (payroll$_i$ [in millions of dollars]/class count$_i$), implying that small firms are more likely to benefit from rate suppression. This finding suggests that any advantage of large firm size due to lower costs of self-insurance is, on average, offset by the greater political advantage of smaller firms, which are presumably more frequently locally owned.

Of the state variables, the ratio of filed to approved rates is strongly and positively related to residual market shares.[22] Contrary to expectations, both current and lagged growth in statutory benefits are negatively related to residual market shares. This relationship could reflect correlation with other omitted state characteristics or reverse causal-

---

22. The t-statistics on the state variables may be upward biased because of correlation in unobserved characteristics across classes in the same state (Moulton 1990). We have not attempted to adjust for this potential bias; in this case, however, the t-statistics are sufficiently large that they are likely to be significant even after such adjustment.

ity; that is, statutory changes to reduce benefits were enacted in states with high residual market shares.

Of the eighteen industry dummies, eight are significantly negative, and the remainder are insignificant relative to agriculture (the omitted class), suggesting that agriculture is an unusually large beneficiary of rate suppression. Adding industry fixed effects, however, increases the adjusted R-squared by only 3.3 percentage points. This is further evidence that industry is not an important factor in explaining political influence.

The results are similar when the residual market share of risks is substituted as the dependent variable, with the important exception that the dominant class indicator (risks$_i$ divided by the mean value of risks) is significantly negative. Recall that the share of class payroll in the residual market includes the payroll from all firms that employ that class, whereas the residual market share of risks is an unweighted count of the residual market share of firms that have this class as their dominant class. The difference in results suggests that dominant classes have less political influence when they account for relatively small share of payroll.

Loss-ratio tests of between-class cross-subsidies. Between-class cross-subsidies should lead to differences in loss ratios between classes.[23] Table 6–2 reports regressions for the log of the three-year mean loss ratio marketwide (voluntary plus residual markets) for each class for the twenty-seven states for which five years of data are available.[24] Lagged values are used for explanatory variables that are poten-

23. In principle, differences in expected loss ratios might be a better indicator of between-class cross-subsidies than differences in residual market share. In practice, however, expected loss ratios are not observable, and realized loss ratios are highly variable at the class level (see below).

24. The log transform gives less weight to extreme values of the loss ratio, which probably reflect stochastic shocks rather than accurate observations on the expected value to which the theory pertains.

TABLE 6–2
BETWEEN-CLASS SUBSIDIES AND STATEWIDE (VOLUNTARY AND RESIDUAL MARKETS) LOSS RATIO (LOG), IN TWENTY-SEVEN STATES
(absolute t-statistics with White standard error in parentheses)

Variable	Equation 1, No Fixed Effects	Equation 2, Industry Fixed Effects	Equation 3, State and Industry Fixed Effects
Intercept	0.103 (0.859)	0.184 (1.449)	−1.022 (8.805)
Log (loss per claim$_i$) ($t-1$)	0.091 (8.458)	0.087 (7.528)	0.089 (7.082)
Log (claim frequency$_i$) ($t-1$)	0.127 (11.175)	0.139 (10.669)	0.141 (10.559)
Risks$_i$ / $\overline{\text{risks}}$ ($t-1$)	0.243 8.665	0.023 (8.229)	0.031 (0.701)
Payroll$_i$ / $\overline{\text{payroll}}$ ($t-1$)	−0.001 (1.209)	−0.002 (1.469)	0.090 (0.940)

Log (payroll$_i$ / risk$_i$) (t–1)	0.033	0.039	0.041
	(5.201)	(5.035)	(4.668)
Statutory growth (t–1)	0.535	0.381	—
	(0.627)	(0.443)	—
Herfindahl	–0.216	–0.203	–0.136
	(3.187)	(2.976)	(2.105)
(Risks$_i$ / $\overline{\text{risks}}$) × R (t–1)	—	—	–0.008
	—	—	(0.191)
(Payroll$_i$ / $\overline{\text{payroll}}$) × R (t–1)	—	—	–0.092
	—	—	(0.958)
Adjusted R^2	0.036	0.040	0.111

NOTE: Subscript i denotes class level variable. Overstrike denotes access class.
SOURCE: Authors.

tially endogenous. The first equation includes only class-specific variables; the second equation includes industry fixed effects; the third equation adds state fixed effects and includes two interacted variables to test whether the effect of the relative influence variables is greater in heavily regulated states. The heavy regulation indicator, R, is defined as one for states in the top third of the distribution of residual market shares, zero otherwise.

The low adjusted-R^2 reflects the extreme variation even in the class-specific loss ratios, even after taking a log transform of the three-year means. Nevertheless, some variables are significant and consistent with predictions. The classwide loss ratio is significantly and positively related to lagged claim frequency and to claim severity. Since these variables are predictors of high expected future loss costs, these findings are consistent with the hypothesis of systematic subsidies to high risks (classes with relatively high pure premium) or relatively low wages per employee. These findings are also consistent with the evidence from the residual market share analysis.

Loss ratios are positively related to mean firm size (log (payroll/risk) $(t-1)$)), as expected assuming that large firms have lower expense loadings and that their better options for self-insurance protect them from being taxed. Loss ratios are significantly higher for classes with a relatively large number of risks, consistent with the prediction that classes that are frequently the dominant class in a firm would benefit from regulation.[25] Loss ratios are not significantly related to relative class payroll. These effects are not consistently different between states with heavy rate suppression and less regulated states.

---

25. This positive association between relative risks and loss ratios, in contrast to the insignificant or negative association with residual market shares, could reflect the tendency for greater skewness and hence higher mean losses in classes with a relatively large number of small firms.

To measure the effect of class concentration in relatively few states, we include a Herfindahl index that reflects the distribution of class payroll across states. A high value of the index indicates that the payroll of that class is concentrated in relatively few states. The coefficient of the Herfindahl index is negative, implying that more diffuse classes have higher loss ratios. This is consistent with the hypothesis that mobility across states protects a class against excessive rates.

Adding industry fixed effects has a negligible effect on the adjusted R^2, confirming that any industry effects are not strongly consistent across states. State fixed effects add only an additional seven percentage points.

Within-Class Cross-Subsidies. Within-class cross-subsidies can affect the relative competitive position of firms within an industry. The incentives to achieve within-class cross subsidies are probably negligible for diffuse classes that are employed in many industries but are rarely the dominant class, such as clerical workers. For classes that account for a significant fraction of payroll for the firms that employ them, however, distortions of within-class rates may influence the competitive position of different firms in the industry.

Within-class cross-subsidies can be achieved by suppression of experience rating, by suppression of residual market rates, and by regulation of voluntary market rate relativities to influence the allocation of the residual market deficit across voluntary market classes. As summary measures of within-class cross-subsidies from the voluntary market to the residual market in a class, we analyze the relation between voluntary and residual market premiums and loss ratios.[26]

---

26. Harrington (1990) uses a similar analysis of premium differences. Our analysis here focuses on average cross-subsidies; it does not attempt to measure cross-subsidies between employers in the residual market.

Voluntary market premiums. As noted, any increase in voluntary market prices within a class to subsidize the state-wide residual market deficit might be viewed as consistent with some degree of within-class cross-subsidy if some firms insured in the residual market within the class are subsidized because of rate suppression. For the purpose of analyzing within-class cross-subsidies, however, it is useful to define a within-class cross-subsidy as arising when the voluntary market premiums for a specific class bear a disproportionate share of the residual market deficit for that class. The voluntary market premium for class i in state j in period t, P_{ijvt}, can be written as a function of own expected loss costs L_{ijvt}, the competitive expense loading l, the percentage rate suppression in the voluntary market m, the lagged statewide residual market deficit D_{jt-1}, and the lagged class-specific residual market deficit D_{ijt-1}:

$$P_{ijvt} = (\lambda - \mu)L_{ijvt} + \gamma\,(R_{ijvt}/R_{jt})D_{jt-1} + (\delta - \gamma)D_{ijt-1} \quad (6\text{--}1)$$

where γ is the percentage pass-through to voluntary market premiums of the statewide residual market deficit, (R_{ijvt}/R_j) is class i's voluntary market share of total payroll in state j, and δ is the pass-through rate for class i's own residual market deficit. If $\delta - \gamma > 0$, a disproportionate share of the residual market deficit in a class is shifted to the voluntary market risks in that class, resulting in within-class cross-subsidies. Dividing through by voluntary market payroll R_{ijvt} yields [27]

$$P_{ijvt}/R_{ijvt} = (\lambda - \mu)L_{ijvt}/R_{ijvt} + \gamma D_{jt-1}/R_{jt} + (\delta - \gamma)D_{ijt-1}/R_{ijvt} \quad (6\text{--}2)$$

27. In the denominator we use voluntary rather than total market payroll under the assumption that lagged residual market deficits can at most be passed on in current rates of the voluntary market.

We estimate the class-specific share of the residual market deficit using the class-specific share of residual market payroll:

$$D_{ijt-1} = D_{jt-1} R_{ijrt-1} / R_{jrt-1}$$

Table 6–3 reports estimates of equation 6–2 for the log of the premium to payroll dollar ratio for the voluntary market in period A and for the growth in the premium to payroll dollar ratio between periods A and B. The actuarial variables have the expected effects: premiums are positively related to expected losses, as estimated by the lagged loss ratio, and negatively related to mean payroll per firm (payroll$_i$/class count$_i$), as expected given the inverse relation between expense loading and payroll. Controlling for these actuarial variables, several indicators of political influence have expected effects. The pass-through of residual market losses includes a significantly positive class-specific component, in addition to the mean statewide component, in both the premium levels and premium growth equations. This evidence is consistent with the hypothesis of within-class cross-subsidies.

Premiums are significantly lower for classes with a relatively large payroll and significantly higher for diffuse classes, consistent with the theory of political influence and with earlier results. Premium levels are lower for dominant classes. Industry fixed effects reduce but do not eliminate the significance of these class-specific characteristics. Premium growth is positively related to contemporaneous benefit change but negatively related to lagged benefit change, possibly because of correlation with other, omitted state characteristics.

Loss ratio differences. A second measure of within-class cross-subsidies is the difference between the loss ratios for the residual and voluntary markets. Suppression of residual market rates increases the residual market loss ratio,

TABLE 6–3
VOLUNTARY MARKET PREMIUM LEVELS AND GROWTH
(absolute t-statistics using White standard errors in parentheses)

Variable	Log (Premium / Payroll)[a]		Growth in Premium/Payroll[a, b]	
	Equation 1	Equation 2	Equation 1	Equation 2
Intercept	6.687	9.286	0.144	0.179
	(2.249)	(3.291)	(1.318)	(1.694)
Log (loss$_i$ / payroll$_i$) $(t-1)$	0.495	0.437	0.008	0.007
	(13.819)	(12.111)	(7.412)	(5.819)
Log (payroll$_i$/class count$_i$) $(t-1)$	−0.114	−0.115	−0.002	−0.001
	(6.318)	(6.434)	(2.925)	(0.852)
Risks$_i$/ $\overline{\text{risks}}$ $(t-1)$	−0.117	−0.092	−0.000	−0.000
	(7.679)	(7.619)	(0.786)	(1.059)
Class count$_i$/ $\overline{\text{class count}}$ $(t-1)$	0.067	0.034	−0.001	−0.001
	(3.313)	(2.222)	(2.491)	(2.361)

Payroll$_i$ / $\overline{\text{payroll}}$ (t–1)	–0.059	–0.028	0.001	0.001
	(3.535)	(2.294)	(3.209)	(2.792)
Statewide deficit (t–1)	69.512	113.947	7.687	8.257
	(1.495)	(2.647)	(5.063)	(5.487)
Class deficit (t–1)	17.603	20.858	0.847	1.372
	(2.545)	(2.155)	(2.395)	(5.326)
Statutory benefit growth (t–1)	–0.904	–1.221	0.066	0.057
	(1.790)	(2.453)	(3.911)	(3.600)
Statutory benefit growth	–5.529	–7.816	–0.153	–0.194
	(2.178)	(3.140)	(1.752)	(2.214)
Adjusted R^2	0.691	0.726	0.275	0.284

a. Industry fixed effects in second equation only.
b. [Premium / payroll]$_t$ – [premium / payroll]$_{t-1}$.
SOURCE: Authors.

whereas pass-through of the resulting deficit tends to decrease the voluntary market loss ratio.

Table 6–4 reports equations for the loss ratio difference.[28] The loss ratio difference is positively related to the difference in expected claim costs, as estimated by the difference in the lagged (log) loss per $100 payroll. Controlling for this difference in expected costs, the loss ratio difference is significantly positively related to rate suppression in the state, as measured by the lagged class-specific residual market share; however, this variable is insignificant after controlling for state fixed effects. The loss ratio difference is negatively related to mean firm size, as expected if large firms have less incentive to engage in political pressure since they have the option of self-insurance. The other measures of political influence are not significant at conventional levels.

Conclusions

There is strong evidence that rate regulation in workers' compensation results in persistent cross-subsidies at three levels: between classes within a state; between low- and high-risk employers within classes in a state; and to policyholders statewide, presumably from insurer equity. The analysis here has focused on between- and within-class cross-subsidies but has shown that these increase as statewide rate suppression increases. The patterns of cross-subsidies are consistent with predictions from a simple model of political influence. High-risk and possibly low-wage workers are generally beneficiaries because of higher stakes and possibly less opposition. Relatively large classes generally benefit from rate suppression. There is some evidence that

---

28. We use statewide rather than submarket-specific measures of most of the explanatory variables, because of concern for endogeneity bias even with the lagged values of variables that change little across years, such as class count and firm size.

TABLE 6–4
WITHIN-CLASS CROSS-SUBSIDIES AND LOSS RATIO DIFFERENCE (LOG)
(absolute *t*-statistics using White standard errors in parentheses)

Variable	Log (Loss/Premium) r − Log (Loss/Premium) v	
	Equation 1	Equation 2
Intercept	1.183	1.750
	(3.381)	(0.350)
D log (loss$_i$ / $\overline{\text{payroll}_i}$) (t−1)	0.208	0.215
	(4.656)	(4.809)
Risks$_i$/ $\overline{\text{risks}}$ (t−1)	−0.013	−0.016
	(0.909)	(1.107)
Payroll$_i$ / $\overline{\text{payroll}}$ (t−1)	0.007	0.006
	(1.487)	(1.376)
Class residual market share (t−1)	0.610	−0.020
	(3.117)	(0.084)
Log payroll$_i$ / class count$_i$ (t 1)	0.085	−0.111
	(2.589)	(3.294)
Alabama	—	−0.115
	—	(1.263)
Florida	—	0.058
	—	(0.690)
Georgia	—	−0.361
	—	(4.455)
Louisiana	—	−0.084
	—	(0.857)
Maine	—	0.244
	—	(1.330)
Michigan	—	−0.437
	—	(4.117)
Adjusted R^2	0.089	0.112

NOTE: Dependent variable = log (residual market loss ratio) − log (voluntary market loss ratio). With industry fixed effects.
SOURCE: Authors.

classes that are diffuse within a state tend to be losers. Small firms are beneficiaries, presumably because of advantages in local influence or because small employers, with immobile capital, have greater personal stakes in influencing outcomes. Industry effects are generally weak. State-specific effects, however, are strong. Understanding the forces that lead to such severe regulation in some states remains an important topic for future research.

7
Policy Implications

Our empirical analysis is consistent with the hypothesis that rate suppression increases claim costs for workers' compensation by distorting the incentives of employers, employees, and insurers. With the available data, we cannot distinguish how far this reflects an increase in the frequency, severity, and duration of injuries and how far it reflects increased claims filing and the amount paid with little effect on real injury rates. Both effects raise significant policy concerns, although increases in real injury rates are obviously of greatest concern. The purpose of the workers' compensation system is to deter injuries and compensate efficiently for those that do occur. If, as our evidence suggests, the workers' compensation program is actually generating unnecessarily high injury-related costs due to the regulation of rates for workers' compensation insurance, this outcome is clearly counterproductive, and it significantly undermines the already tenuous case for rate regulation.

The cost-increasing effects of rate regulation may have been reduced in the 1990s as a result of voluntary and residual market rate increases and changes in pricing programs for the residual market. These changes have increased rate surcharges for employers with poor loss experience and have reduced the size of residual markets and deficits. Our finding that rate suppression increases costs nonetheless remains important. Residual markets in some states are still large by historical standards. Moreover, the basic structure of rate regulation that depressed rates in the face of upward pressure on claims costs in the 1980s through the early 1990s remains intact in many states. Insurers face considerable uncertainty about the growth in residual markets, residual market deficits, and voluntary market burdens. The regulatory system in many states remains vulnerable to significant deterioration from a recurrence of rapid growth in claim costs, a return to rate suppression, and exacerbated cost growth.

This concluding chapter discusses methods of further reducing the cost-increasing effects of rate regulation. Most important, our evidence that rate suppression increases costs provides considerable support for further dismantling traditional systems of prior approval rate regulation and allowing workers' compensation insurance rates to be determined by competition rather than by regulation. We also provide brief comments on (1) replacing residual markets with state provision of coverage, which has occurred in several states and has been proposed in others, and (2) requiring self-insurers to contribute toward residual market deficits, which has been suggested in some states. While recent favorable experience has reduced the pressure for these proposals, this lull may be short-lived if rapid cost growth returns. We also briefly discuss the possible use of explicit tax-based subsidies to fund residual market deficits.

Improving Incentives for Cost Control

Market incentives for cost control in states with large residual markets and prior approval rate regulation could be enhanced by actions that simultaneously increase residual market rates and provide increased flexibility for insurers to charge rates in the voluntary market that are commensurate with the expected cost of providing coverage. These changes would substantially eliminate the cost-increasing effects of rate regulation, depopulate the residual market, and provide greater equity between firms.

Under the current structure of regulation that persists in many states, voluntary market rates remain too low to induce voluntary market supply for many employers. With two-tiered rates (higher residual market rates than voluntary market rates), residual market rates are too low for some employers insured in the residual market and possibly too high for others. Without more flexibility in voluntary market pricing, insurers are unwilling to supply coverage voluntarily to employers for whom the residual market rate is too high. In addition, because residual market rates are too low for some employers, the residual market tends to crowd out the voluntary market even if insurers have the flexibility to charge higher voluntary market rates to these employers.[1] Thus, both greater flexibility in voluntary market prices and higher (and perhaps more flexible) residual market rates are needed to depopulate the residual market.

Existing takeout programs for the residual market in some states provide insurers with limited flexibility to remove risks from the residual market. These programs allow an insurer that voluntarily insures a business previously in the residual market to do so without having the voluntary premium volume increase its residual market assessment for several years. While takeout programs reduce the price needed for an insurer to write coverage voluntarily, they provide no incentive to write residual market business voluntarily when the voluntary market rate is insufficient to cover costs exclusive of the discounted value of any residual market assessments. Moreover, the time limit (for example, three years) might be insufficient to allow the insurer to recoup the upfront costs of writing some business voluntarily. Market assistance programs (MAPs) might

---

1. Applications to the residual market often must include the names of two insurers that have declined to offer coverage. This requirement could be met even if a number of insurers were willing to provide coverage voluntarily. If employers seek the lowest premium, some will find their way to the residual market even if some insurers would insure voluntarily at a higher rate.

facilitate the matching of employers that are searching for coverage with insurers willing to write them in the voluntary market. Publication of lists of employers in the residual market might also be useful, although agents have, in some cases, resisted the publication of such lists.

Another source of flexibility in the current system is the ability of insurers in many states to deviate from NCCI loss costs. In principle, insurers could apply for higher rates, perhaps for coverage sold through an affiliate or subsidiary, which would allow some residual market business to be insured voluntarily. The requirement that percentage deviations be uniform across classes, however, limits flexibility in a number of states. In addition, insurers might find it difficult or impossible to justify upward deviations in an environment in which regulators are facing pressure for low rates from employers.

Finally, current schedule rating systems used in many states with prior approval regulation provide some flexibility to charge higher rates in the voluntary market to employers that are perceived as having a greater risk in a given class. Schedule rating, however, often cannot be applied to small employers that are not subject to experience rating. Moreover, the maximum permissible schedule rating credits may be insufficient to induce an insurer to provide coverage voluntarily in many instances.[2]

Competitive Rating. Whether comprehensive regulation of voluntary market rates (and rate classes) in workers' compensation insurance is desirable has been debated at length during the past fifteen years (for example, GAO 1986; Klein

---

2. Two-tiered rates encourage the use of schedule rating. With uniform rates for the voluntary and residual markets, schedule rating surcharges would increase rates above the residual market rate, and the business would probably obtain coverage through the residual market. With higher residual market rates, schedule rating could allow insurers to charge rates in between the residual market rate and the standard voluntary market rate.

1992; Klein, Nordman, and Fritz 1993). In our view, the evidence strongly suggests that competitive rating is both more efficient and, in some ways, more equitable than heavy rate regulation. Because the workers' compensation insurance market is structurally competitive (see Klein, Nordman, and Fritz 1993), there is no need for rate regulation as a constraint on market power. In most states, many insurers sell coverage, and a few firms do not dominate the market. Barriers to entry for new insurers or for existing insurers that wish to expand into other states are generally low. Thus, competition and the option of self-insurance can be expected to prevent excessive rates and profits. For this reason, some states have switched to some form of competitive rating in which insurers are allowed substantial flexibility in pricing individual employers and in changing rates over time without prior approval of regulators.

The simplest and best method of providing increased flexibility in voluntary market pricing would be for more states to adopt *true* competitive rating, that is, competitive rating laws that rely on competition rather than on rate regulation. The least comprehensive change in this regard would allow insurers to file and use new rates without prior approval by state regulators.[3] Existing rate classes, experience rating systems, and rules regarding advisory organizations could be maintained. To be fully effective, insurers would have to be assured that filed rates would not be challenged and disapproved after they were put into effect. This

---

3. Some states implement so-called competitive rating laws in a manner similar to prior approval. As noted in earlier chapters, the term *competitive rating* has sometimes been used broadly to describe prospective loss-cost systems and laws that allow insurers to deviate from advisory rates or loss costs even though prior regulatory approval of rates and advisory loss costs is required. These laws do not constitute true competitive rating. The NAIC competitive model rating law allows disapproval of rates only if the commissioner demonstrates that there is lack of competition. Advisory loss costs should also not be subject to prior approval.

assurance would require specific legislative protection or a clear change in philosophy toward reliance on competition to regulate rates.

Adoption of competitive rating would have four main advantages:

1. Competitive rating would encourage the voluntary market supply of coverage at rates commensurate with expected claim costs, thus eliminating the distorting effects of voluntary market rate regulation. This would reduce the size of the residual market. Our evidence indicates that claim cost growth would be lower if more employers were insured voluntarily.

2. Competitive rating would allow any employers currently insured in the residual market at excessive rates— rates in excess of costs and their proportionate share of the residual market deficit—to be insured in the voluntary market at lower rates.

3. Competitive rating would reduce uncertainty for insurers concerning the adequacy of future prices to cover costs. This reduction in uncertainty would reduce the price necessary for insurers to invest in infrastructure needed to provide quality coverage. It would encourage insurers to make new investments in infrastructure and to maintain existing infrastructure, discourage exit by existing insurers, and encourage entry by new insurers.

4. With competitive rating, competition among insurers would protect employers from rates in excess of amounts needed to cover expected costs and would provide insurers with a reasonable return on investment. Competition also would discourage inferior service.

The expected deficit in the residual market might increase with the adoption of competitive rating unless residual market rates were simultaneously increased (see below). This increase could occur as certain employers— those currently insured in the residual market at rates in excess of their expected costs plus a proportionate share of the discounted expected cost of the residual market deficit—begin to be insured at lower rates in the voluntary market. Since the voluntary market share would increase, however, any increase in the burden on employers already insured in the voluntary market should be modest.

Three arguments might be made for comprehensive prior approval regulation of rate classes, rate levels, and experience rating plans for workers' compensation insurance despite the advantages of competitive rating:

1. Rate regulation might facilitate valuable cooperative activity through insurance advisory organizations, such as the NCCI. As discussed in chapter 2, advisory organizations collect data, estimate future claim costs, and file rates or loss costs on behalf of insurers in most states. These cooperative activities offer considerable potential cost savings for insurers. Some observers argue, however, that these activities provide a mechanism for anticompetitive behavior and hence should be substantially limited if rates are not subject to strict regulatory oversight. Possible limits on these activities in conjunction with the adoption of competitive rating might make it more costly for insurers to estimate loss costs. Small insurers might have greater difficulty competing.

2. Some argue that government should provide close regulatory oversight over rates when it mandates the purchase of insurance (or establishes requirements for self-insurance). Allowing competition to regulate rates for mandatory insurance, however, is not logically inconsistent and may be economically advantageous if the market is structurally competitive. Usually, the view that the government should regulate the prices of the goods or services that it requires employers or citizens to buy presumes that unregulated prices would be excessive. This outcome, however, would not occur in a well-functioning competitive market. Moreover, this view tends to ignore the distorting

and cost-increasing effects of rate regulation that have been documented here.

    3. Some persons may support subsidies to certain high-risk activities and low-wage workers on equity grounds.

    Our study has not directly addressed some of these possible advantages of prior approval rate regulation. Our evidence that rate suppression increases costs, however, significantly strengthens the case for competitive rating. Our evidence also shows that regulation subsidizes high-risk activities. If cross-subsidies to some high-risk activities or low-wage workers are deemed socially desirable, such subsidies might be achieved through other, less distorting and more transparent means. Given the evidence here of cross-subsidies through the rate regulation process and the resulting cost-increasing effects and questionable equity of the distributive effects, there is clearly a case for more careful and explicit consideration of what subsidies are deemed socially appropriate and how they are to be implemented. We return to this below.

Self-sustaining Residual Market Rates. The second key component of a policy designed to eliminate substantially the cost-increasing effects of regulation and depopulate residual markets is to approve residual market rates at self-sustaining levels (that is, at levels commensurate with the expected cost of insuring employers in the residual market) as lower-risk employers in the residual market are insured voluntarily, thus putting upward pressure on the residual market deficit. In conjunction with adopting competitive rating for the voluntary market (or otherwise significantly increasing insurer flexibility in establishing voluntary market rates), residual market rate increases would have several desirable effects, including (1) a further decline in the size of the residual market and residual market deficits; (2) a decline in existing subsidies to employers with the highest expected claim costs, thus improving their incentives to

148

reduce risk; and (3) a reduction in the proportion of the market that is subject to possible suboptimal incentives for cost control that may occur when insurers pool residual market operating losses.

Alternative Methods of Financing Subsidies

If subsidies to high risks are an intended policy objective despite their cost-increasing effects, then alternative methods of financing these subsidies should be considered: (1) replacing the residual market with a state fund, (2) requiring self-insurers to contribute toward the deficit, and (3) using tax-based subsidies to fund the residual market deficit.

Replacing the Residual Market with a State Fund. Over twenty states have a state fund that provides some coverage to the private sector. During the 1990s, a number of states created state funds to replace the residual market in response to earlier residual market growth and deficits (for example, Texas and Louisiana). Under this approach to addressing residual market problems, the state fund could guarantee coverage at rates set by the state to any employer that experienced difficulty in obtaining coverage from private insurers. Private insurers presumably would not be responsible for financing any deficit on business insured by the state fund.

Creation of state funds to replace residual markets is not needed if the policy objective is to produce a healthy voluntary insurance market and to shrink the size of the market that is not insured voluntarily. If, despite the cost-increasing effects of rate suppression, the objective of a state is to subsidize the cost of workers' compensation to make the system more affordable for some employers, the effects of replacing the residual market with a state fund depend on its design.

If voluntary market insurers do not have to contribute toward any deficit for the state fund, the voluntary market burden would be eliminated, and there would be fewer distortions in the voluntary insurance market. Subsidies might also be targeted more accurately to intended recipients. The total market would separate into two parts: a voluntary market with self-sustaining rates (assuming that voluntary market rate regulation allowed adequate rates) and a state market with rates below expected claim and other costs to make coverage more affordable to targeted employers. The method ultimately used to finance the deficit in the state fund (for example, general tax revenues or surcharges on all employers) might produce less costly distortions in behavior than with traditional residual markets.[4]

There would be significant drawbacks, however, to replacing the residual market with a state fund to subsidize the costs of coverage for some employers. Experience suggests a risk of state funds expanding significantly and thus further crowding out supply by private insurers and increasing cost growth and the resources ultimately needed to finance subsidies. Considerable pressure also could arise to expand the subsidy to additional employers, and a large unfunded deficit could result, in part due to the cost-increasing effects of regulation.

Another problem is that creation of a state fund would not necessarily create a healthy voluntary market. Regulation of rates for the voluntary market could still discourage insurers from expanding the supply of voluntary market coverage. In addition, insurers would need to consider the likelihood that they would eventually be required to contribute to deficits for the state fund. An increase in the unfunded liability for the state fund and the amount of cash needed to pay current claims could create significant pressure for making insurers contribute.[5] When deciding

---

4. If the state fund were operated on a cash flow basis, assessments might not be needed for a number of years following its creation (cf. Harrington 1992).

5. This problem occurred with the residual market for workers' compensation in Maine and the residual market for auto insurance in New Jersey.

how much business to insure voluntarily, rational insurers will consider the likelihood and risk that they will be asked to pay later.

Yet another issue is whether incentives for collecting premiums and controlling claim costs would differ substantially if a state fund were created to replace the residual market. It is not clear whether accountability of state funds (which might utilize private servicing carriers) to state legislatures would increase or decrease any problems compared with traditional mechanisms for the residual market, but incentives for claim cost control and premium collection might be lower than under current arrangements with private monitoring.

Requiring Self-Insurers to Contribute toward the Deficit. Proposals have periodically been made to require self-insurers to contribute toward residual market deficits. If the policy objective is to reduce the cost-increasing effects of rate regulation, shrink the residual market, and produce a healthy voluntary insurance market, requiring self-insurers to contribute toward deficits would not appear to serve a useful purpose. But if the objective of a state is to subsidize the cost of complying with the workers' compensation system through residual market rate regulation—in an attempt to make the system more affordable for some employers despite the cost-increasing effects of rate suppression—then making self-insurers contribute toward the deficit might have several advantages.[6]

A possible advantage of assessing self-insurers if residual market deficits are large is that it might significantly expand the base for recovering residual market deficits and

---

6. Requiring self-insurers to help fund residual market deficits might require significant structural changes in the residual market plan of operation. It might, for example, make sense to allow self-insurers to participate in the NCCI pool. If so, self-insurers might need to be given input concerning the selection, remuneration, and monitoring of servicing carriers.

thus reduce the burden on employers that buy coverage in the voluntary market. Some representatives of self-insurers have argued that they should not be required to subsidize commercial insurance companies, but this argument misses a key point. Over time, if the voluntary market is to remain viable, expected residual market deficits must be funded by employers insured in the voluntary market, assuming that no direct tax-financed subsidies are used. Assessing self-insurers would make them share the burden of subsidizing employers that pay inadequate residual market rates. The implicit tax rate in premium rates for the voluntary market that is necessary to fund a given deficit would decline. The incentive for employers to self-insure to avoid this implicit tax would also decline. The possibility of a voluntary market collapse under an adverse scenario might decline as well.

From a political perspective, increasing the base for recovering deficits by assessing self-insurers could increase deficits by reducing political pressure for approving residual market rates at self-sustaining levels. If so, requiring self-insurers to contribute toward the deficit might also increase the size of deficits and the cost-increasing effects of cross-subsidies. Whether this would be true depends on whether the net political pressure for holding rates below costs for some employers increases or decreases if self-insurers become more involved in the process.

Tax-based Subsidies to Fund the Residual Market Deficit. Assuming that there is an explicit policy decision to subsidize some employers, a third alternative is to use the existing, private forms of residual markets but to fund any deficit from general revenues of the state or from a broad-based, earmarked tax. An advantage of this approach is that it makes transparent the size of the subsidies, the beneficiaries, and the funding. A possible disadvantage is that spreading the costs of financing subsidies more broadly could lessen political pressure against subsidies. An evaluation of this form of direct financing—relative to the current system of indirect financing through higher premiums for other employers and possibly expanded to include self-insurers—is beyond the scope of this study. A few states have used this approach to fund deficits in high-risk pools for health insurance.

Conclusions

Our empirical analysis is consistent with the hypothesis that rate suppression is counterproductive in that it increases claim costs over time. Although the data do not permit us to distinguish the extent to which this reflects an increase in injury rates or an increase in claim costs for a given injury rate, both are cause for concern. These findings support the case for policies that would help control claim costs by restoring incentives for efficient cost control. One necessary policy change would be to provide insurers with greater pricing flexibility in the voluntary market. The simplest and best method of accomplishing this goal would be to adopt true competitive rating laws that rely on competition to determine rates rather than on rate regulation. A second necessary change would be to approve residual market rates at self-sustaining levels (that is, at levels commensurate with the expected cost of providing coverage to employers insured in the residual market). Many existing regulatory systems and some proposed modifications would retain rate suppression for significant numbers of higher-risk employers, with an attendant increase in costs. In contrast, providing greater pricing flexibility through true competitive rating laws so that rates can adjust to reflect costs offers the potential to benefit large numbers of employers and employees, with gains in efficiency and equity.

References

Appel, David, Michael McMurray, and Mark Mulvaney. 1992. "An Analysis of the Net Costs of Workers' Compensation Insurance." New York: Milliman and Robertson.

Baumol, William J. 1991."Technological Imperatives, Productivity and Insurance Costs." *Geneva Papers on Risk and Insurance* 16:154–65

Becker, Gary. 1983. "A Theory of Competition among Pressure Groups for Political Influence." *Quarterly Journal of Economics* 98: 371–400.

Blackmon, B. Glenn, Jr., and Richard Zeckhauser. 1991. "Mispriced Equity: Regulated Rates for Auto Insurance in Massachusetts." *American Economic Review* 81 (2): 65–69.

Bruce, Christopher, J., and Frank J. Atkins. 1993. "Efficiency Effects of Premium Setting Regimes under Workers' Compensation: Canada and the United States." *Journal of Labor Economics* 11(1), pt. 2: S38–69.

Butler, Richard J. 1994. "Economic Determinants of Workers' Compensation Trends."*Journal of Risk and Insurance* 61 (3): 383–401.

Butler, Richard J., and John D. Worrall. 1990. "Premium and Loss Cycles in Workers' Compensation." In *Benefits, Costs, and Cycles in Workers' Compensation,* edited by Philip Borba and David Appel, 129–62. Boston: Kluwer Academic.

———. 1991. "Claims Reporting and Risk-Bearing Moral Hazard in Workers' Compensation Market." *Journal of Risk and Insurance* 60(2): 185–207.

———. 1993. "Self-Insurance in Workers' Compensation." In *Workers' Compensation Insurance: Claim Costs, Prices and Regulation,* edited by David Durbin and Phillip Borba, 129–46. Boston: Kluwer Academic.

Carroll, Anne M. 1993. "An Empirical Investigation of the Structure and Performance of the Private Workers' Compensation Market." *Journal of Risk and Insurance* 60(2): 185–207.

———. 1994. "The Role of Regulation in the Demand for Workers' Compensation Self-Insurance." *Journal of Insurance Regulation* 13(2): 168–84.

Carroll, Anne M., and Robert Kaestner. 1995. "The Relationship between Regulation and Prices in the Workers' Compensation Insurance Market." *Journal of Regulatory Economics* 8(2): 149–66.

Cheadle, A., G. Franklin, C. Wolfhagen, J. Savarino, P. Liu, C. Salley, and M. Weaver. 1994. "Factors Influencing the Duration of Work-related Disability: A Population-based Study of Washington State Workers' Compensation." *American Journal of Public Health* 84 (2): 190–96.

Chelius, James R., and Karen Kavanaugh. 1988. "Workers' Compensation and the Level of Occupational Injuries." *Journal of Risk and Insurance* 55(2): 315–23.

Chelius, James R., and Robert S. Smith. 1987. "Firm Size and Regulatory Compliance Costs: The Case of Workers' Compensation Insurance." *Journal of Policy Analysis and Management* 6(2): 193–206.

Cummins, J. David, Scott E. Harrington, and Robert M. Klein. 1991. "Cycles and Crises in Property/Casualty Insurance." In *Cycles and Crises in Property/Casualty Insurance: Causes and Implications for Public Policy* , edited by J. David Cummins, Scott E. Harrington, and Robert W. Klein, 1–51. Kansas City, Mo.: National Association of Insurance Commissioners.

Danzon, Patricia M. 1987. "The Political Economy of Workers' Compensation Benefit Structures." Wharton School, Health Care Systems Dept., University of Pennsylvania.

———. 1988. "The Political Economy of Workers' Compensation: Lessons for Product Liability." *American Economic Review* 78 (2): 305–10.

———. 1989. "Mandated Employment-based Health Insurance: Incidence and Efficiency Effects." Wharton School, Health Care Systems Dept., University of Pennsylvania.

———. 1992. "Administrative Costs, Price Regulation and Efficiency: A New Look at Old Issues." Paper presented at the National Council on Compensation Insurance Conference on Workers' Compensation Issues, November.

Fields, Joseph A., and Emilio C. Venezian. 1991. "Medical Cost Development in Workers' Compensation." *Journal of Risk and Insurance* 58(3): 497–504.

Fishback, Price V., and Shawn Everett Kantor. 1995. "Did Workers Pay for the Passage of Workers' Compensation Laws?" *Quarterly Journal of Economics* 110(3): 713–42.

Fortin, Bernard, and Paul Lanoie. 1992. "Substitution between Unemployment Insurance and Workers' Compensation: An Analysis Applied to the Risk of Workplace Accidents." *Journal of Public Economics* 49(3): 287–312.

Gogol, Daniel. 1985. "The Much Greater Profitability of New York Workers' Compensation Risks with Higher Modifications." *Journal of Risk and Insurance* 52(1): 151–56.

Gruber, Jonathan, and Alan B. Krueger. 1990. "The Incidence of Mandated Employer Provided Insurance: Lessons from Workers' Compensation Insurance." Princeton Industrial Relations Section Working Paper, November, 279: 47.

Harrington, Scott E. 1984. "The Impact of Rate Regulation on Prices and Underwriting Results in the Property-Liability Insurance Industry: A Survey." *Journal of Risk and Insurance* 51(4): 577–623.

———. 1988a. "The Relationship between Standard Premium Loss Ratios and Firm Size in Workers' Compensation Insurance." In *Workers' Compensation Insurance Pricing*, edited by David Appel and Philip Borba, pp. 109–44. Boston: Kluwer Academic.

———. 1988b. "Regulation and Subsidies in Automobile Insurance." College of Business Administration, University of South Carolina.

———. 1990. "The Relationship between Voluntary and Involuntary Market Rates and Rate Regulation." *Journal of Risk and Insurance* 57(1): 9–27.

———. 1992. "Presidential Address: Rate Suppression." *Journal of Risk and Insurance* 59(2): 185–202.

Harrington, Scott E., and Helen I. Doerpinghaus. 1993. "The Economics and Politics of Automobile Insurance Rate Classification." *Journal of Risk and Insurance* 60(1): 59–84.

Harvey, A. C. 1976. "Estimating Regression Models with Multiplicative Heteroscedasticity." *Econometrica* 44: 461–65.

Hofflander, Alfred E., Blaine F. Nye, and Jane D. Nettesheim. 1992. "A Comparative Evaluation of Workers' Compensation Rating Laws." Stanford Consulting Group, Menlo Park, Calif.

Hunt, H. Allan, Alan B. Krueger, and John F. Burton, Jr. 1988. "The Impact of Open Competition in Michigan on the Employers' Cost of Workers' Compensation." In *Workers' Compensation Insurance Pricing*, edited by David Appel and Philip Borba, pp. 109–44. Boston: Kluwer Academic.

Hunter, Robert J. 1993. "Rate Suppression and Its Consequences: A Critique." *Journal of Insurance Regulation* 11(3): 333–43.

Hyatt, D., and B. Kralj. 1995. "The Impact of Workers' Compensation Experience Rating on Employer Appeals Activity." *Industrial Relations* 34(1): 95–106.

Kahley, William J., and Tanya E. Restrepo. 1993. "Profitability and the Assigned Risk Market." National Council on Compensation Insurance, Boca Raton, Fla.

Klein, Robert W. 1992. "Regulation, Competition, and Profitability in Workers' Compensation Insurance." *John Burton's Workers' Compensation Monitor* 5(2): 7–20.

Klein, Robert W., Eric C. Nordman, and Julienne L. Fritz. 1993. "Market Conditions in Workers' Compensation Insurance." National Association of Insurance Commissioners, Kansas City, Mo.

Kralj, B. 1994. "Employer Responses to Workers' Compensation Experience Rating." *Relations Industrielles–Industrial Relations* 49 (1): 41–61.

Kramer, Orin S. 1992. "Rate Suppression, Rate-of-Return Regulation, and Solvency." *Journal of Insurance Regulation* 10 (4): 523–63.

Krueger, Alan B. 1990. "Incentive Effects of Workers' Compensation Insurance." *Journal of Public Economics* 41 (1): 73–99.

Krueger, Alan B., and John F. Burton, Jr. 1990. "The Employers' Costs of Workers' Compensation Insurance: Magnitudes, Determinants, and Public Policy." *Review of Economics and Statistics* 72(2): 228–40.

Meyer, Bruce D., W. Kip Viscusi, and David L. Durbin. 1995. "Workers' Compensation and Injury Duration: Evidence from a Natural Experiment." *American Economic Review* 85(3): 322–40.

Mixon, Franklin G., Jr., and Rand W. Ressler. 1993. "An Empirical Note on Union Influence of Workers' Compensation Payments." *Rivista Internazionale di Scienze Economiche e Commerciali* 40(9): 805–12.

Moore, Michael J., and W. Kip Viscusi. 1990. *Compensation Mechanisms for Job Risks: Wages, Workers' Compensation, and Product Liability.* Princeton: Princeton University Press.

Moulton, Brent R. 1990. "An Illustration of a Pitfall in Estimating the Effects of Aggregate Variables on Micro Units." *Review of Economics and Statistics* 72: 334–38.

National Association of Insurance Commissioners. 1993. "Survey of Servicing Carriers." Minutes of the Residual

Market Working Group of the Workers' Compensation (D) Task Force, September 20, 1993.

National Council on Compensation Insurance. *Management Summary.* 1982–1994 eds. Boca Raton, Fla.: NCCI.

————. 1993. *Annual Statistical Bulletin.* Boca Raton, Fla.: NCCI.

————. 1996. *1996 Issues Report.* Boca Raton, Fla.: NCCI.

Nelson, William J., Jr. 1993. "Workers' Compensation: Coverage, Benefits, and Costs, 1990-91." *Social Security Bulletin* 56(3): 68–74.

Pauly, Mark V., Paul Kleindorfer, and Howard Kunreuther. 1986. "Regulation and Quality Competition in the U.S. Insurance Industry." In *The Economics of Insurance Regulation,* edited by Jorg Finsinger and Mark Pauly. London: Macmillan Press.

Peltzman, Samuel. 1976. "Toward a More General Theory of Regulation." *Journal of Law and Economics* 19(2): 211–40.

Priest, George. 1987. "The Current Insurance Crisis and Modern Tort Law." *Yale Law Journal* 96: 1521–90.

Ruser, John W. 1985. "Workers' Compensation Insurance, Experience Rating, and Occupational Injuries." *RAND Journal of Economics* 16(4): 487–503.

————. 1991. "Workers' Compensation and Occupational Injuries and Illnesses." *Journal of Labor Economics* 9(4): 325–50.

————. 1993. "Workers' Compensation and the Distribution of Occupational Injuries." *Journal of Human Resources* 28(3): 593–617.

Schmidle, Timothy P. 1995. "The Impact of Insurance Pricing Deregulation on Workers' Compensation Costs." *John Burton's Workers' Compensation Monitor* 8 (5): 1–12.

Shavell, Steven. 1982. "On Liability and Insurance." *Bell Journal of Economics* 13(1): 120–32.

Stigler, George. 1971. "The Theory of Economic Regulation." *Bell Journal of Economics and Management Science* 2(1): 3–21.

U.S. General Accounting Office. 1986. "Initial Experience with Competitive Rating." Washington, D.C.: Government Printing Office.

Viscusi, W. Kip, and Michael J. Moore. 1987. "Workers' Compensation: Wage Effects, Benefit Inadequacies, and the Value of Health Losses." *Review of Economics and Statistics* 69(2): 249–61.

Index

About the Authors

PATRICIA M. DANZON is the Celia Moh Professor of Health Care Systems and Insurance at the Wharton School of the University of Pennsylvania. She has held positions at the University of Chicago, Duke University, and the RAND Corporation.

The author is a fellow of the Institute of Medicine and the National Academy of Social Insurance. She has been a consultant on international health care issues to the World Bank, the New Zealand government, the Asian Development Bank, and the U.S. Agency for International Development.

Ms. Danzon received a B.A. from Oxford University and a Ph.D. in economics from the University of Chicago. She has been widely published in the fields of health care, insurance, and liability systems. The author is an adjunct scholar of the American Enterprise Institute.

SCOTT E. HARRINGTON is professor of insurance and finance and Francis M. Hipp Distinguished Faculty Fellow in the College of Business Administration, University of South Carolina. He was on the faculty of the Wharton School from 1978 to 1988.

Mr. Harrington is the associate editor of the *Journal of Risk and Insurance* and the *Journal of Financial Services Research*. His articles have been published in journals such as the *Journal of Business, Journal of Banking and Financing, Journal of Insurance Regulation, Science, Regulation,* and *Review of Economics and Statistics.* Mr. Harrington is the coeditor of four books, including *Foundations in Insurance Economics:*

Readings in Economics and Finance. He is a former president of the American Risk and Insurance Association and of the ARIA Risk Theory Society.

He received his Ph.D. in finance from the University of Illinois in 1979.

A NOTE ON THE BOOK

This book was edited by Ann Petty
of the publications staff
of the American Enterprise Institute.
The index was prepared by Julia Petrakis,
and the figures were drawn by Hördur Karlsson.
The text was set in New Baskerville.
Cynthia Stock of Silver Spring, Maryland, set the type,
and Edwards Brothers, of Lillington, North Carolina,
printed and bound the book,
using permanent acid-free paper.

The AEI Press is the publisher for the American Enterprise Insti-
tute for Public Policy Research, 1150 Seventeenth Street, N.W.,
Washington, D.C. 20036; *Christopher C. DeMuth,* publisher; *Dana
Lane,* director; *Ann Petty,* editor; *Leigh Tripoli,* editor; *Cheryl
Weissman,* editor; *Jennifer Lesiak,* production manager.